Contents

Introduction

There are many parts of Great Britain renowned for their charm or beauty – the Cotswolds, the Cornish coast, the Scottish Highlands to name just a few – but it is generally agreed that the Lake District is the jewel in England's crown. With its wide variety of attractions, it may sound like a cliché, but there really is something to appeal to everyone.

Its most obvious draw is the landscape. The mountains, lakes, vales, valleys and rolling countryside attract hordes of walkers, hikers, climbers and mountaineers to its heart year after year, and the number of books – from local publications to the most famous Wainwright guides (*see p54*), which

Great Langdale, enclosed by the fells

detail every nook and cranny of the national park and around – are astonishing for such a small region. The Lake District National Park was established in 1951 to preserve the area from development, which in turn has enabled it to become one of the most profitable tourist regions in the country. It almost feels as if every second house is a bed and breakfast, opening its doors to one visitor after another keen to put on a pair of wellies or walking boots and burst out into the great outdoors.

Again, for an area of its size, the Lakes have a remarkable literary heritage that has not only influenced Britain but the rest of the world. Two of the finest poets of the 19th century, William Wordsworth and Samuel Taylor Coleridge (*see pp44–5*), found their inspiration in the surrounding countryside here, while probably the best loved children's author of all time, Beatrix Potter (*see pp22–3*), metamorphosed the wildlife around

A view down Derwentwater, which has several islands

her into characters that are adored by children and adults the world over. And how many people, messing about in boats on one of the 16 lakes in the area, are reliving their childhood memories of reading Arthur Ransome's *Swallows and Amazons*, which fictionalised the area that the author loved so much?

History certainly hasn't bypassed Cumbria either. The Romans had several settlements here, and their most impressive British landmark, Hadrian's Wall – stretching along the English-Scottish border from the Solway Firth to Northumbria – is one of the country's most visited sights. The Vikings, too, have left their mark in places, and for centuries Cumbria, like its Northumbrian neighbour, suffered under the many battles and skirmishes that were ongoing in the English attempt to seize the Scottish throne, and the Scots' attempt to hang on to it. The border reivers (*see pp66–7*) also caused havoc, with clannish families

from both sides of the border raiding and rampaging with total disregard for law and order. The 18th and 19th centuries also saw enormous changes: Cumbria was one of the heartlands of England's mining industry, the arrival of the railways saw the rise of new towns and wealth as well as the arrival of the first tourists, and the coastal location meant that ports were kept busy exporting local minerals and importing goods such as tobacco and rum from the Americas. All these aspects of Cumbria's history can be uncovered in various excellent museums and preserved sights.

So, whether it's for a long weekend or a more extended stay, with its abundance of fresh air activities and plenty of attractions in which to take cover on an inevitable rainy day, the Lake District and Cumbria offer the choice between either an action-packed or a revitalising peaceful holiday destination.

The region

It's all in the name – the Lake District. A combination of naturally formed lakes, with a striking backdrop of mountains, hills, woods and forests, that draws visitors year after year to take in the breathtaking scenery and tranquil setting.

The landscape beckons you to sport your walking boots and scale the heights to be able to look down over the lakes and vales beneath you, but if that sounds too energetic simply sit back and absorb this wonderful area from the luxury of a lakeland cruise. Enjoy the top-of-the-range hotels or personal service offered by the hundreds of bed and breakfasts.

Geography

Although there is still evidence of slate in the Lake District that dates back 500 million years, the region as we see it today was formed during volcanic activity around 400 million years ago that created the sandstone and limestone mountains. England's highest mountain, Scafell Pike (*see pp51–3*), is a clear remnant of these early volcanoes.

Walkers admiring the view at Ashness Bridge, near Keswick

Aira Force Falls near Ullswater

The lakes and valleys were primarily formed during the last Ice Age. There are 16 lakes in the area, although only one, Bassenthwaite, bears the actual word 'lake' in its title. Given the watery and mountainous landscape, there are inevitably plenty of impressive waterfalls in the region, as well as caves and crags. The natural minerals that are available in the area – slate, graphite, limestone, coal and iron ore (haematite) – greatly contributed to the economic success of the region in the 18th, 19th and 20th centuries, although Cumbria has always been and remains a predominantly agricultural county with highly successful sheep- and cattle-rearing farmsteads.

Traditionally this is an area of woodland and forests, but the fact that many place names now bear the word 'thwaite' is an indication of how important agriculture is to the region – dating from Viking times, the word describes a forest that has been felled in order to make way for farming land.

(*Cont. on p11*)

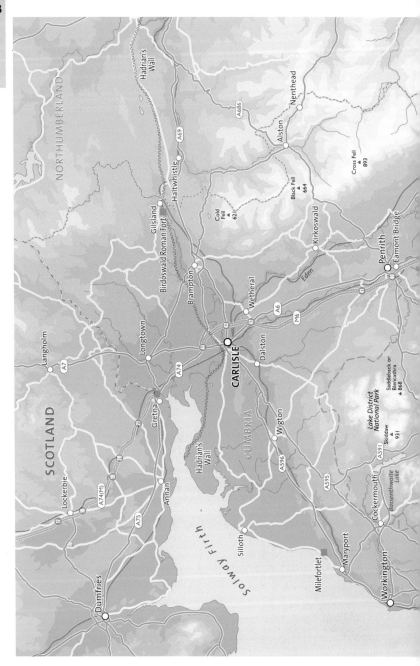

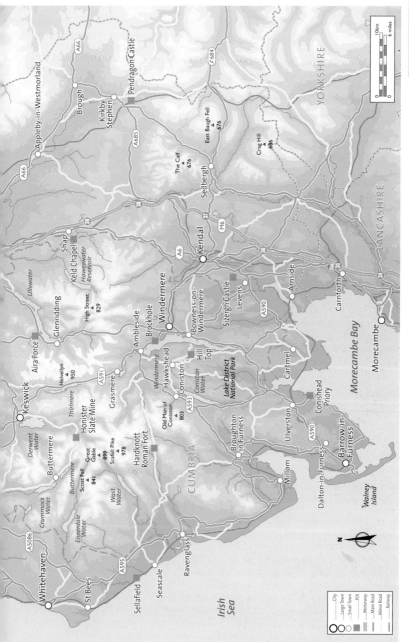

Irish Sea

Morecambe Bay

Lake District National Park

CUMBRIA

LANCASHIRE

YORKSHIRE

Whitehaven
St Bees
Sellafield
Seascale
Ravenglass
Millom
Dalton-in-Furness
Walney Island
Barrow-in-Furness
Conishead Priory
Ulverston
Broughton-in-Furness
Cartmel
Morecambe
Carnforth
Arnside
Levens
Sizergh Castle
Bowness-on-Windermere
Windermere
Kendal
Brockhole
Ambleside
Hawkshead
Coniston
Hill Top
Grasmere
Honister Slate Mine
Keswick
Buttermere
Glenridding
Aira Force
Shap
Keld Chapel
Brough
Kirkby Stephen
Appleby-in-Westmorland
Pendragon Castle
Sedbergh
Hardknott Roman Fort

Crummock Water
Ennerdale Water
Wast Water
Derwent Water
Thirlmere
Buttermere
Ullswater
Haweswater Reservoir
Coniston Water
Windermere

Scoat Fell ▲ 841
Great Gable ▲ 899
Scafell Pike ▲ 978
Old Man of Coniston ▲ 803
Helvellyn ▲ 950
High Street ▲ 829
The Calf ▲ 676
East Baugh Fell ▲ 676
Crag Hill ▲ 686

A66
A685
A683
A6
A684
A5086
A595
A591
A593
A590
A6
M6
B6

○○○ City ─ Large Town ─ Small Town ■ POI ═══ Motorway ═══ Main Road ······· Minor Road ─── Railway

10km
6 miles

N

The beaches, here at St Bees, also draw visitors

Flora and fauna

The predominant trees in the Lake District are oaks and ash, although yews, elms and conifers feature in abundance, too. Heather and moss also grow in upland areas. Among the wildflowers and plants that visitors can expect to see are snowdrops (January and February), ferns, meadowsweet, valerian, primroses, bluebells and daffodils (about which Wordsworth wrote one of his most famous poems).

The most common animals that will be seen here are sheep, particularly the Herdwick breed (*see p118*), which are agile and hardy enough to cope with the mountainous and rocky landscape of the fells. They are invariably herded not just by local farming shepherds but also by faithful sheepdogs, of the collie breed. The red squirrel was once a common sight in these parts but sadly is now under threat by the non-indigenous grey squirrel, so a lot of conservation work is being undertaken to protect the former.

The coastal region to the west, with its marshes and mudflats, is ideal for birdwatchers – barnacle geese, oystercatchers, plovers and mallards are common sights. Inland, skylarks, merlins and woodcocks can be sighted, while in the higher regions birds of prey such as buzzards and peregrine falcons take to the skies.

The coastal area used to be a prime fishing area but this has gone into decline in recent years. In the lakes and rivers, however, there is an abundance of salmon, trout and pike, and rare species such as vendace and Arctic char. There is a vast number of designated fisheries that allow anglers to get the most out of the area (*www.lakedistrictfishing.net*).

Politics

The most prominent issue for the Lake District, in both natural and man-made features, is conservation. The main charitable institutions that preserve individual sites are the National Trust (itself established in Cumbria), the Forestry Commission and English Heritage. These three organisations, plus a few smaller ones, put a great deal of time, effort and finance into preserving the Lake District's spectacular landscape

OSPREYS

For centuries, ospreys, beautiful large birds of prey, were a regular sight in the United Kingdom but were driven to extinction by the mid-19th century. However, one of the great success stories, in ornithological terms, is the return of the species to the Lake District in 2001. Two ospreys were spotted nesting by Bassenthwaite Lake and have returned here every summer since, observed and watched over by the Lake District National Park Authority. Ospreys typically spend the winter in Africa and the summer in Europe. The young are incubated almost entirely by the female, while the male takes on the parental role once the eggs have hatched, teaching the young to fish for food. For a chance to glimpse these extraordinary birds, there is a summer (April to September) viewpoint at Dodd Wood as well as an exhibition at the Whinlatter Visitor Centre near Keswick (*www.ospreywatch.co.uk*).

as well as its many historic buildings, from Roman sites to places such as Wordsworth's birthplace (*see p34*) or Beatrix Potter's farmhouse (*see p50*). Cumbria County Council also keeps a close eye on issues that may affect the area, such as afforestation.

The Lake District National Park Authority has also ruffled a few feathers in recent years by limiting boating speeds on Windermere and Coniston Water to 16km/h (10mph). While this has little effect on gentle dinghy or canoe sailing, or the slow-moving cruisers that take tourists from one end of the lakes to the other, it has upset many powerboaters and waterskiers. However, the argument is that the slower speeds help to retain a more peaceful atmosphere.

Cumbria has always been an agricultural region but farming throughout England has had a hard time for many years, and Cumbria was particularly badly affected by the foot and mouth epidemic in 2001 when so much livestock had to be slaughtered. There are now a number of projects in place that offer grants and subsidies to farmers in the hope that this will allow them to keep one of the county's most important sources of income in place.

One of the mainstays of the fell farmers is their sheep count and the annual lambing season, and this became an issue in 2005 when the government announced a UK-wide ban on fox-hunting. Rather than being an aristocratic sport as it is in the less agricultural regions in southern England, fox-hunting was a fairly important activity in Cumbria, to cull the foxes that regularly invade fields

The Forestry Commission looks after much of the woodland in the region

Sheep grazing by Grasmere

and kill new-born lambs. There was widespread dissent among farmers, who felt that the ban was appealing to the sentiments of people who had no understanding of country life but nevertheless the controversial ban was put in place and any hunts that take place today, do so illegally.

Another perennially controversial issue in Cumbria is the presence of the Sellafield Nuclear Power Station (*see p107*). While many agree that this enormous plant offers widespread employment for the area, there are questions about its safety record, with many serious or near miss incidents occurring in its history, as well as general discomfort about the need for any nuclear plant at all. There have been ongoing investigations into whether there are higher statistics of

cancers such as leukaemia among the population living close to the plant, and as recently as 2007 an official inquiry began as to whether tissue from deceased former Sellafield workers was removed for medical study without permission.

Another heated debate is about whether to introduce a congestion charge for drivers on the region's busy roads. Locals fear that this will only have a detrimental effect on them and on small businesses, while the fair majority of the cars on the roads may belong to tourists. So far, no final decision has been made, but it is yet another issue that is causing unrest.

This may be one of the most beautiful and peaceful pockets of England, but it seems that politics are never far from the scene.

History

c. 6000 BC   Neolithic people begin to inhabit the landscape, evidenced by stone weapons excavated, dating from this time.

2000–700 BC   Bronze takes over from stone for producing weapons and tools, and early agricultural practices begin.

300 BC   The Celts (Cymry) arrive from other parts of the country, predominantly Wales, and bring with them a new language and more sophisticated methods of farming, with iron tools, and a system of government. The main tribe in the Cumbrian region is the Brigantes.

AD 69   The Romans reach northern England and construct Hadrian's Wall between England and Scotland (*see pp16 & 60*).

c. 550   St Kentigern (also known as St Mungo) passes through on his journey from Scotland to Wales – the first evidence of Christianity in the area.

664   The Angles (Anglo Saxons) arrive in the area from Northumbria.

925   Viking settlers arrive and begin to farm the uplands, giving the region names that remain today, such as dale, fell and thwaite.

945   King Edmund defeats the Celt warlord Dunmail and annexes the area to King Malcolm I of Scotland.

1092   Following the Norman Conquest of 1066, King William II takes control of Carlisle, and various castles are built in the region as the battle for control between Scotland and England ensues over centuries.

1237   The Treaty of York 'officially' establishes the border between England and Scotland, with Cumbria firmly on the English side. The region begins to gain wealth with sheep farming and the wool trade.

1296   John Balliol of Scotland invades Cumbria but is

defeated by Edward I. Further wars between England and Scotland continue, with William Wallace and Robert the Bruce defending the north of the border against kings Edward I and Edward II. Centuries of strife lead to an anarchic society that is largely 'ruled' by the border reivers (*see pp66–7*).

1603 The Union of the Crowns makes James VI of Scotland also King James I of England, creating a united Great Britain.

1770s Writers and artists begin to discover the Lake District, and books about its beauty are published, encouraging a burgeoning tourist industry.

1799 William Wordsworth (*see pp44–5*) moves to Dove Cottage and, along with fellow poets Samuel Taylor Coleridge and Robert Southey, depicts the beauty of the region in his works.

1847 The first passenger railway service opens between Kendal and Windermere, allowing considerably easier access to the region.

1895 Canon Rawnsley forms the National Trust in the Lake District, to which Beatrix Potter (*see pp22–3*) would leave all her land.

1947 Construction begins of Windscale Nuclear Plant (later named Sellafield).

1951 The Lake District National Park is formed, protecting the area from development and conserving its beauty.

1974 Cumberland, Westmorland, Furness (Lancashire) and Sedburgh (Yorkshire) are joined together in the official administrative county of Cumbria.

2001 Cumbrian farmers are the worst hit by the foot and mouth crisis that sweeps across Britain's livestock.

2006 The release of *Miss Potter*, a film about the life of Beatrix Potter, brings more tourists to the Lake District.

2008 *Mr Bhatti*, a Bollywood comedy set in the Lake District, is released.

2010 The BBC plan to release a new film of *Swallows and Amazons*.

The Romans

Prior to the arrival of the Romans, the Celts were the ruling force in Cumbria, but they were soon to find themselves competing against the mighty force of an empire that was already covering much of western Europe. Already established in the south for a couple of decades, the Romans reached northern England in AD 69 and wasted little time in making their presence felt.

The Romans' main base in northern England was in York but they eagerly set up several auxiliary posts in the northwest, primarily with the ambition of moving into Scotland under the guidance of the Roman governor in England, Agricola. They set about constructing roads in the area, linking the various forts they established in order to maintain military and political control. Many of those roads, such as the Stanegate between Carlisle and Northumberland, and the road between Ambleside and Brougham (known as the High Street), still exist. Remains of many of the forts, which typically each occupied a landscape of around 2ha (5 acres), to include barracks, lookouts and more, can also still be seen today. Partial walls, gatehouses and remnants of a bathhouse are evident at Hardknott Fort, near Eskdale (*see p117*), which remains a striking vision against the mountain backdrop, while even more impressive because of the extent of their survival are the ruins of the bathhouse at Ravenglass (*see pp105–7*), where individual rooms can still be clearly defined between the high walls.

Other Roman ruins can be found at sites around Penrith and in Maryport, where a Roman museum displays fascinating pieces excavated from local sites (*see p108*). Tullie House in Carlisle also has excellent exhibits

The Roman bath house at Ravenglass dates from the 1st century AD

Hardknott Roman Fort, near Eskdale

detailing Roman history in the area (*see p58*). Another contribution to the area was the introduction of more sophisticated and successful agricultural practices, which brought a greater economic value to the area.

Ultimately the Romans were never really able to get a foothold in Scotland, apart from a few minor southern ventures. The native Caledonians (or Picts) did not prove as easily won over as the English and were more experienced warriors in their mountain terrain – which led to the famous Hadrian's Wall, built to protect the southern communities from precisely those they had tried to overrule (*see pp60–61*).

The Romans were a force in the area for more than 300 years, but by the 5th century AD, the great empire was in decline and they returned to Europe and the various problems that awaited them there. The region fell back into the hands of the Celts and, before long, it was taken over by the new invaders, the Saxons.

Culture

As a predominantly rural district, Cumbria and the Lakes don't have the great art centres that can be found in many other parts of the country, but its beauty has certainly attracted more than its fair share of world-renowned artists and writers: some resident, some visiting. In summer the region is also alive with many highly popular arts and music festivals (see pp24–5). All that fresh air, too, has evidently played tricks for centuries on active imaginations, and it's not short of the odd legend or two.

Art

Surprisingly, given its beautiful and dramatic scenery, the Lake District has attracted remarkably few world-renowned artists in its history, but it did not escape the notice of Britain's finest landscape painter JMW Turner (1775–1851). He visited the region in 1797 and applied his masterful oils on to canvas to convey both Coniston Water and, more famously, Buttermere Lake, now part of the Tate collection. The Romantic painter John Constable (1776–1837) is best known for his landscapes of southern England, but he did visit the Lakes in 1806, producing lovely watercolours of Windermere, Keswick and Borrowdale.

In the 20th century the most notable artist in the area was the German Dadaist Kurt Schwitters (1887–1948), best known for his large-scale installations known as *Merzbau* (or simply *Merz* for short). Schwitters had considerable success in his native Germany, as well as in the United States, but was forced to flee the Nazis in 1937, going first to Norway, then to England. Following internment on the Isle of Man until the end of World War II, Schwitters settled in Ambleside in 1945 where he began work on his final installation, the 'Merzbarn', consisting of a variety of found or salvaged objects. Part of the original barn is still standing (although the artwork is now on display in Newcastle) and Schwitters was buried in Ambleside cemetery.

Of course, the beauty of the Lakes has always drawn a large number of both amateur and professional artists. Today the **Lake Artists Society** (*www.lakeartists.org.uk*), established in 1904, is still going strong. Members must be resident in Cumbria and an annual summer exhibition of works in the New Hall in Grasmere is an established event on the Lakes' calendar.

Theatre

The best known theatre in the Lake District is the aptly named **Theatre**

by the Lake in Keswick
(*www.theatrebythelake.com*). It not only
has a year-round programme of
cultural gems, from theatrical classics,
to modern plays, to drama, but also
plays host to several festivals such as
the Keswick Jazz Festival (*see p24*).
The Sands Centre in Carlisle
(*www.thesandscentre.co.uk*) is a popular
venue for a wide range of cultural
performances, from ballet, opera,
touring West End productions, classical
and popular music and stand-up
comedy. Other notable theatres in the
region are The Kirkgate in
Cockermouth and The Old Laundry
Theatre in Bowness-on-Windermere.

The Theatre by the Lake in Keswick

Cinema

Given its beauty, it's not surprising
that the Lake District draws film
location scouts to its landscape on a
regular basis. The most recent and
probably the most influential film on
the region was the 2006 biopic *Miss
Potter*, starring Renée Zellwegger as
Beatrix Potter. Yew Tree Farm in
Coniston was used as a replica of her
real home, Hill Top (*see pp23 and 50*),
the offices of her publisher were filmed
in Whitehaven, while various
landscapes, including Loweswater and
Derwentwater can be seen in all their
glory on celluloid. The bleak, dank
cottage in which Withnail and his
friend find themselves on holiday 'by
mistake' in the cult classic 1987 film
Withnail and I is in Wet Sleddale, just
south of Penrith, although much of the
rest of their time in the Lakes was
actually filmed in southern England.

In terms of going to see such films
on the big screen, there are cinemas at
Penrith, Cockermouth, Workington,
Kendal and a lovely 1930s refurbished
cinema at Ulverston, as well as
multiplexes in Carlisle.

Literature

The literary giants that are most
readily associated with the Lake District
are the Lake Poets Wordsworth,
Coleridge and Southey (*see pp44–5*),
the art critic John Ruskin (*see p37*), and
the children's favourites Beatrix Potter
(*see pp22–3*) and Arthur Ransome (*see
p41*). But other wordsmiths, past and

present, have also translated the beauty of the area on to the written page.

Although New Zealand-born, the novelist Hugh Walpole (1884–1941) lived most of his adult life at Brackenburn Lodge at Catbells, from where he wrote his famous *Herries Chronicles* from 1930 onwards. A native Cumbrian, Margaret Forster (b.1938) is a prolific novelist and biographer who still lives in the Lake District. Among her best known works are the novel *Have the Men Had Enough* and the memoir of her own Cumbrian family over the centuries, *Hidden Lives*. She is married to another writer, Hunter Davies (b.1936), also Cumbrian-born and passionate about the area. He has written a number of books about his home region, including biographies of William Wordsworth and Alfred Wainwright, although he is probably best known for his books about the 1960s pop phenomenon The Beatles.

Writer and broadcaster Melvyn Bragg was born in Wigton in 1939 and sets a number of his novels in Cumbria, including *The Maid of Buttermere* (1987) and *A Time to Dance* (1990). The Lakes seem to attract children's authors too, perhaps because of the freedom and seeming innocence allowed by the rural landscape. One-time Kendal resident John Cunliffe set his stories about Postman Pat (and his black and white cat) in fictitious places that were all inspired by real Cumbrian villages.

Folklore and Legends

Like almost every other corner of Great Britain, Cumbria and the Lake District are rife with folkloric tales, ghosts and legends. Many of these stem from Roman and Viking times, when superstition preceded science in most cases and, prior to the arrival of Christianity, a belief in evil spirits that could cause disease, harm crops and more, were a common manner of approaching the trials and tribulations of rural life. Fairies, who could be kindly or capricious, depending on their treatment, were a strongly held belief, and there are so-called 'fairy sites' at Hardknott Pass (*see p117*) and Elva Hill, near Bassenthwaite Lake. There is a stone circle and at Beetham, where legend has it anyone who can descend the steep stone steps unsupported will have a wish come true.

King Arthur and his legendary knights also feature prominently in local tales. Most notable of these is Eamont Bridge (*see p72*) where there is not only an ancient earthwork called King Arthur's Round Table, but a cave where Sir Lancelot is said to have murdered the resident giant. Long Meg and Her Daughters at Little Salkeld, just north of Penrith, is another stone circle dominated by a megalith (Long Meg). The story goes that the stones were originally witches, punished for their deeds by being turned to rock, but that anyone who can count the stones more than once and come out with the same total will bring the witches back to life

King Arthur's Round Table at Eamont Bridge

– an unlikely event since some of the stones are now underground and many are doubtless missing. Long Meg itself is supposed to 'bleed' if damaged in any way – all such superstition assisting conservation organisations invaluably.

One of the more entertaining, if certainly far-fetched tales in Cumbrian folklore, however, dates from more recent times. In the 19th century two brothers and their sister lived in a house called Croglin Grange, just northeast of Penrith and next door to a graveyard. One night, the sister saw bright lights flitting around in the grounds but carried on up to bed. Some time later a macabre figure, with two lights for eyes, broke in through the bedroom window and pounced, causing the woman to let out a blood-curdling scream. The brothers arrived to the rescue to find the invader gone but their sister bleeding profusely from bites to her neck. After recovering from the ordeal, the family decided that they would try and capture this strange being, using the sister to tempt him back. While this succeeded in theory, he duly returning for his night-time snack, the brothers shot him and he managed to escape again. The next morning, an even more terrifying discovery was made – the church crypt was full of human bones, and open coffins, except for one, which contained the sleeping 'vampire', complete with bullet wound. The family, assisted by the rest of the village, burned both body and coffin, and the 'phantom of Croglin Grange' was destroyed for good.

Beatrix Potter

Intrinsically associated with the Lake District through her children's stories and artworks of mischievous ducks, rabbits, squirrels and other local creatures, Beatrix Potter (1866–1943) reached a whole new level of fame when her life story was brought to the screen by Renée Zellwegger in the 2006 film *Miss Potter*. The region, too, had no less a starring role with locations such as Derwentwater (*see p47*) and Coniston (*see p37*) providing a stunning cinematic backdrop that has brought a flock of visitors to the area to take in these landscapes for themselves – several companies now offer Beatrix Potter tours on the back of the film.

Although a Londoner by birth and upbringing, Beatrix was heavily influenced by the many childhood holidays spent with her family in first Scotland, then the Lake District, revelling in the nature that surrounded her. At home she had pet rabbits and other animals to whom she was devoted and as an adult would also become a respected botanist, particularly in the study of fungi.

Her literary and artistic talents and aspirations were apparent from an early age but were largely dismissed

Mrs Tiggywinkle at the World of Beatrix Potter in Bowness-on-Windermere

Mrs Tiggywinkle (hedgehog), Jeremy Fisher (frog), Tom Kitten and Jemima Puddleduck, to name just a few, have been entertaining children and adults alike for more than 100 years and show little sign of abating.

Passionately devoted to the Lake District all her life, Beatrix used royalties from her books to buy the farm Hill Top in 1905 (*see p50*), and subsequent land in the area, moving permanently to the Lakes in 1913 when she finally married a solicitor named William Heelis, much of whose work was spent attempting to protect local landowners and farmers from wealthy industrialists wishing to buy up and modernise the district. Beatrix, too, was zealous about conservation of the area and became a respected and prize-winning breeder of Herdwick sheep, native to Cumbria.

Hill Top Farm, bought by Beatrix Potter in 1905

by her aristocratic parents, not least because they considered female careers demeaning. But the determined Beatrix continued to paint and create her animal tales and eventually, in 1902, found an interested publisher, Frederick Warne & Co. Beatrix was involved in many of the publishing decisions, including the insistence that the books be small enough for a young child to comfortably hold (the distinctive pocket-sized books still being published today), and all her instincts proved to be correct. *The Tale of Peter Rabbit* was the first of what would eventually be 23 books that very quickly captured the public's imagination and entered the domain of children's classics. The characters of

Beatrix stipulated in her will that all her land, which was substantial by that time, should be left to the National Trust (an organisation itself set up by Canon Rawnsley, the local vicar who had encouraged Beatrix's talents as a child), which protected it forever from unsympathetic development and was a lasting gift to all those who enjoy the beauty of the region as much as she did. Beatrix's ashes were scattered over an unknown spot in her beloved Lake District, connecting her forever to the land she loved so dearly.

Festivals and events

Outdoor entertainment and live events are a central part of what the Lake District offers visitors, culturally speaking. What it may lack in indoor activities is more than compensated for by the host of cultural engagements – many of which celebrate the region's unique historical traditions – that take place against a backdrop of uninterrupted geographical beauty.

March

Words by the Water, Keswick. A festival of drama productions at the renowned Theatre by the Lake.
Second week.

April

Keswick Film Festival Screenings of films from all over the world at the Alhambra cinema and the Theatre by the Lake, and plenty of talks and film-related events (*www.keswickfilmfestival.org*).
Second weekend.

May

Cockermouth Georgian Festival Celebrating the town's 18th-century heritage with a street market, traditional skills and costumed volunteers (*www.cockermouth.org.uk/georgianfair*).
First weekend.

Keswick Jazz Festival A week-long event with jazz musicians from all over the world descending on Keswick to perform (*www.keswickjazzfestival.co.uk*).
Second week.

Keswick Mountain Festival Walkers, mountaineers and adventurers come to hear talks by some of the great names in these fields, such as Sir Chris Bonnington.
Third week.

June

Appleby Horse Fair One of the oldest horse fairs in the country (*see p78*).
First week.

Boot Beer Festival, Eskdale Locally brewed beers are the main focus, but there is also live music and plenty of other activities (*www.bootbeer.co.uk*).
Early June.

Cockermouth Carnival and Summer Festival A parade of carnival floats kicks off a week of theatre, music and other entertainments.
Last week.

Whitehaven Maritime Festival Vintage ships, aircraft displays, street performers and fireworks are all part of this biennial event (next festival during 2009).
Last week.

July

Furness Tradition Festival, Ulverston
Traditional folk music
(*www.furnesstradition.org.uk*).
Second weekend.

Cumbria Steam Gathering, Grange-over-Sands Historic steam engines and vintage cars, combined with a fair and various food stalls
(*www.steamgathering.org.uk*).
Last weekend.

Maryport Blues Festival Well-known names in the field of blues music, such as Jools Holland, come to perform at this popular event
(*www.maryportblues.co.uk*).
Last weekend.

August

Bank holiday Monday Various country fairs are held in the region, in towns such as Ravenglass.

Mintfest, Kendal A festival of street performers.
Last weekend.

Patterdale Dog Day, Ullswater A traditional sheepdog trial, as well as sheep-shearing competitions, and plenty of other entertainments.
Last weekend.

September

Festival of Books and Drama, Sedburgh Local writers and invited guests celebrate the region's literary heritage.
First two weeks.

Kendal Torchlight Carnival An evening of entertainment on the streets of the town

RUSHBEARING

In the days before church floors were flagstoned, around the end of the 19th century, the ground would be covered with rushes. These rushes were replaced once a year in what were known as rushbearing ceremonies. After the ceremony, in which the entire community took part, gingerbread was the customary snack. Hay, of course, is no longer needed for modern flooring, but five churches in Cumbria still perform the ceremony each July as a mark of their heritage: St Oswald's Church, Grasmere, and St Mary's Church in Ambleside are the most famous.

(*www.kendaltorchlightcarnival.co.uk*).
Second weekend.

Coniston Walking Festival Guided walk (*www.conistonwalkingfestival.org*).
Last weekend.

October

FRED Europe's largest outdoor art festival has installations all over Cumbria.
First week.

November

The Biggest Liar in the World, Santon Bridge In honour of its 19th-century landlord who was famous for his fibs about local life, a competition is held annually at The Bridge Inn to find the person who can tell the most unlikely tale about Cumbria.
Dates vary.

December

Keswick Victorian Fair Locals dress up in costume, and street stalls sell Christmas gifts and mulled wine.
First week.

Highlights

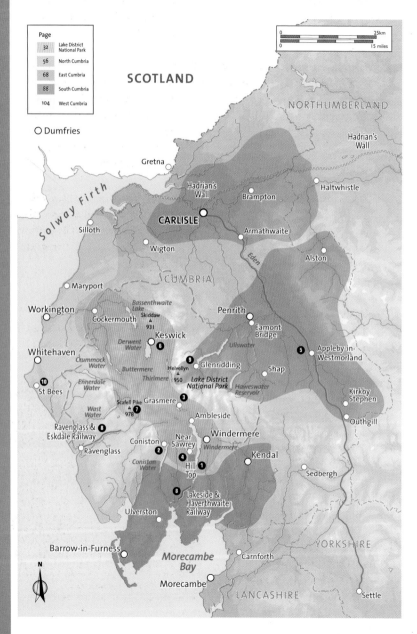

Page

32	Lake District National Park
56	North Cumbria
68	East Cumbria
88	South Cumbria
104	West Cumbria

SCOTLAND

○ Dumfries

Gretna

Hadrian's Wall

Hadrian's Wall

NORTHUMBERLAND

Haltwhistle

Brampton

CARLISLE

Armathwaite

Silloth

Wigton

Eden

Alston

CUMBRIA

Maryport

Bassenthwaite Lake

Penrith

Skiddaw
931

Eamont Bridge

Workington

Cockermouth

Keswick ❻

Derwent Water

Ullswater

Appleby-in-Westmorland ❺

Whitehaven

Crummock Water

Buttermere

Helvellyn
950

❾ Glenridding

Shap

Kirkby Stephen

St Bees ❿

Ennerdale Water

Thirlmere

Lake District National Park

Haweswater Reservoir

Outhgill

Scafell Pike
978 ❼

Wast Water

Grasmere ❸

Ambleside

Ravenglass & Eskdale Railway ❽

Coniston ❷

Near Sawrey ❹

Windermere

Kendal

Ravenglass

Coniston Water

Hill Top ❶

Windermere

Sedbergh

Lakeside & Haverthwaite Railway ❽

Ulverston

Barrow-in-Furness

Morecambe Bay

Carnforth

YORKSHIRE

N

Morecambe

LANCASHIRE

Settle

0 — 25km
0 — 15 miles

Solway Firth

1 Windermere The Lake District's most famous lake offers scenic cruises that ply the water at a genteel pace (*see pp40–42*).

2 Coniston Water Somewhat quieter than Windermere, this is a popular spot for boating, fishing, canoeing and other watersports (*see p37*).

3 Wordsworth country William Wordsworth was born in Cockermouth in a house that is now a museum dedicated to his life (*see p34*). His most famous home, however, is Dove Cottage in Grasmere (*see pp43–6*) where he wrote some his finest works. His masterpiece, *The Prelude*, however, was written at Rydal Mount near Windermere (*see pp40–41*).

4 Beatrix Potter country There are numerous museums devoted to Beatrix Potter's life and work, but the main location is Hill Top Farm in Near Sawrey (*see p50*).

5 Eden Valley Ruined castles, prehistoric and Roman remains, pretty market towns and natural splendours of vales and waterfalls (*see pp76–7*).

6 Keswick Home to the Theatre by the Lake (*see p138*) as well as summer festivals and events (*see pp24–5*).

7 Scafell Pike England's highest mountain is both a draw and a challenge for climbers and hikers (*see pp51 3*).

8 Steam railways A few original railway lines have been preserved as narrow gauge tracks carrying steam trains, such as the Lakeside & Haverthwaite Railway (*see p93*) and the Ravenglass and Eskdale Railway (*see p105*).

9 Hiking trails Tourist offices will have information about local walks, such as Helvellyn from Glenridding, or follow the definitive Wainwright guides (*see p54*).

10 Coastal beaches Cumbria's coastline has a wealth of small resort towns and villages that are well worth exploring, such as St Bees (*see pp114–15*).

Take a cruise on Lake Windermere

Suggested itineraries

Long weekend

They may be the first port of call for all visitors to the area, but Windermere (*see pp40–42*) and Coniston Water (*see p37*) are the quintessence of the Lake District and no first timer should miss them. So if there is only limited time available these are the areas to head to. The longest and deepest of the lakes, Windermere could easily occupy two full days with a variety of cruises that take in some of the many islands while allowing you to absorb the beautiful mountainous landscape above you. Pretty towns such as Ambleside border the lake, as do some impressive houses such as the arts and crafts masterpiece Blackwell. Some striking hotels line the lake, and enjoying a traditional cream tea of scones and jam while looking out over the waters is one of the region's many charms. Literature lovers can also pay a visit to Rydal Mount, one of William Wordsworth's many homes in the Lakes. A few miles over to the west is Coniston Water, which also has literary connections in the figure of John Ruskin. Other than that, in good weather this is a wonderful place to spend a lazy Sunday, taking walks or picnics along the water's edge, hiring a boat, canoe or dinghy from the boating centre, or stepping aboard the steam boat that puffs along the 8km (5-mile) watercourse to only the sound of the lapping of the waves.

One week

A week's holiday should be enough time to see a large proportion of the national park, depending on how much time you want to spend travelling around, or simply spending a few days in one place to take in the landscape. Having 'done' Windermere and Coniston, head to Grasmere and Wordsworth's Dove Cottage (*see pp43–6*), where some of his possessions are on display and a museum details the poet's life. Also don't miss Hill Top Farm (*see p50*) for that other great literary Lakes writer, Beatrix Potter. The children's author did much to conserve her beloved Lake District and gave this farmhouse to the National Trust herself who, according to her wishes, have kept it almost exactly as it was when she resided here.

Keswick (*see pp34–7*) makes an excellent base from which to explore much of the area but is an attractive town in its own right, with plenty of Victorian architecture. However incongruous it sounds, its pencil museum is the main attraction, but for a bit of fun away from all the history and natural beauty, the Cars of the Stars Museum is a terrific collection of motors instantly recognisable from various film and TV shows. Back to Wordsworth in Cockermouth (*see p34*), where the poet's birthplace is another museum that explores aspects of

Beautiful Coniston Water

Rydal Mount, near Ambleside, was Wordsworth's home for almost 40 years

Georgian life. And don't forget to relax after a day's sightseeing with a pint of Jennings ale, locally brewed here. Walkers, of course, will want to get out into the great outdoors, particularly on the northern fells, but make sure safety guidelines are followed (*see p149*) and only those with experience and the right equipment should attempt the main mountain Scafell Pike (*see pp51 & 53*).

Two weeks

A fortnight is enough time to move out of the national park proper and explore the rest of the county of Cumbria. There's plenty of history and some excellent museums in Carlisle (*see pp58–9*), while moving east to Eamont Bridge (*see pp72–3*) and the beautiful Eden Valley (*see pp76–7*) there is everything from Roman ruins, to medieval pele towers (*see pp102–3*), to

ruined castles standing proudly in impossibly romantic settings. And, of course, Hadrian's Wall is one of the greatest sights in the world if history is your thing (*see pp60–61*). For a bit more relaxation take another lake cruise on one of the steamboats that operate on Ullswater (*see p74*). Further south, Kendal (*see pp88–90*) and Ulverston (*see pp95–6*) are lovely towns that again make good bases during explorations in the region, while there are the sands of Morecambe Bay on the border with Lancashire if you want to kick off your shoes and feel the sand between your toes. More sand is on offer along the west coast (*see pp114–15*), where a number of beaches offer relaxation and watersports, while inland in the west of Cumbria are a number of stately homes that have opened their striking rooms and immaculately kept gardens to the public. If time and timetables permit, a ride on one of the steam railways such as the Lakeside and Haverthwaite in the south (*see p93*) and the Ravenglass and Eskdale in the west (*see p105*) should be fitted into the schedule, particularly if children are in tow, as they invariably love these short jaunts through the countryside watching the smoke puffing out of the engine up ahead.

Longer

If you have longer and are intent on exploring, why not head off north of the border into Scotland (*see pp122–3*), either to the main cities of Glasgow or Edinburgh, or the beauties of Loch Lomond and The Trossachs, or simply the coastal villages of the southwest? This border land has been witness to so many disputes in its history that there

are plenty of historical attractions to see. Eastwards lies Northumberland, particularly easy on the South Tynedale Railway or by following the Hadrian's Wall route, or indeed Wainwright's Coast to Coast walk (*see p54*) if you're feeling energetic. Also eastwards are the hills of the Pennines and the North Yorkshire moors, far more wild and windswept than the gentility of the Lake District landscape. One of the best ways to get from Cumbria to Yorkshire if you don't want to drive is on the Carlisle to Settle Railway (*see pp56–7*), an historic route that sometimes still runs steam train excursions for special event days. South lies Lancashire – if you're feeling a bit deprived of human extravagances there is the brashness of Blackpool with its funfair atmosphere and attractions; a greater contrast to the Lakes is difficult to imagine.

Suggested itineraries

The Lakeside & Haverthwaite Steam Railway

Lake District National Park

Covering 2,292sq km (885sq miles), the Lake District is, after the capital London, the most popular place in England. This, of course, has its downsides – traffic jams and crowds during summertime – but with a breathtaking landscape of hills, fells and smaller lakes away from the large hubs of Windermere and Coniston, it's always possible to find a pocket of peace and tranquillity. (See also pages 74–5 for Ullswater and the West Cumbria Section (pp104–19) for the Ravenglass, Eskdale and Ennerdale areas.)

The Lake District was established as a national park in 1951 to preserve its natural beauty, but despite its deserved reputation as a nature-lover's paradise, there really is something to suit everyone here. Water babies will be in their element boating and fishing on the lakes; hikers and mountain climbers are spoilt for choice; bookworms can take in both the landscapes, wildlife and museums that inspired such literary giants as William Wordsworth, Samuel Taylor Coleridge and Beatrix Potter.

Most of the main towns in the area have not only retained their 18th or 19th century charms in the architecture, but are also chock-a-bloc with charming bed and breakfasts. The rest of the national park offers small villages by the lakes or nestling in the hills, backed by farmland that has been worked for centuries and gives a welcome impression of time standing still. If you haven't seen 'the Lakes', you haven't seen England.

COCKERMOUTH

So named because it lies where the River Cocker flows into the River Derwent, this is one of the major towns within the Lake District National Park. It was established in the Middle Ages, as can be seen from the defensive castle (still in private ownership of the Egremont family so closed to the public) and has been thriving ever since, its heyday being the Georgian period, as witnessed by many of the houses from that era. The town is particularly busy each Monday when a weekly market is held, a tradition going back centuries.

Jennings Brewery

Jennings is the most famous brewery in Cumbria and a one-hour tour of their facilities, operational here since the 1870s, will leave you in no doubt as to all the processes that go into making their popular ales, such as Cocker Hoop. You can watch the barley being crushed, hops and yeast being added to the kettles for fermentation, until the

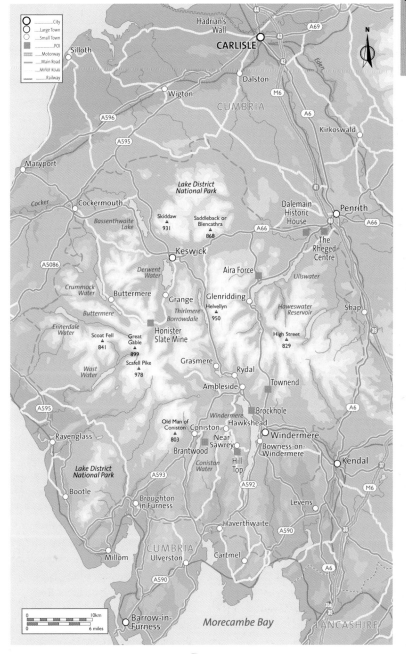

final step when the beer is bottled. At the end of the tour there's a chance to try the ale for yourself in the designated bar area.

Brewery Lane. Tel: 0845 1297185. www.jenningsbrewery.co.uk. Tours Mar–June & Sept–Oct Mon–Sat 11am & 2pm; July–Aug daily 11am & 2pm; Nov–Feb Mon–Fri 2pm, Sat 11am & 2pm. Admission charge.

Wordsworth House

The birthplace of the great Lakes poet William Wordsworth (*see pp44–5*) and his three siblings has been in the hands of the National Trust as a tribute to the man since the 1930s. The Wordsworth family lived here from 1766 until the death of the father, John Wordsworth, in 1783. Today it is a museum but, although there is an obviously strong connection with the poet, the main focus is to portray late 18th-century life in general. As such, all the staff take on roles – maid, cook, servant – in costume and perform duties as they would have done at the time. The kitchen is the most fascinating area of the house, illustrating both cooking methods and ingredients of the period, and there's also a kitchen garden growing produce that would have been used to feed the family in that era. All the other rooms, including living room, bedrooms and offices, have also been furnished authentically.

Main Street. Tel: 01900 820884. www.wordsworthhouse.org.uk. Open: Mar–Oct Mon–Sat 11am–4.30pm. Admission charge.

KESWICK

With its abundance of accommodation options combined with a pretty market town atmosphere, Keswick makes an ideal base for any visit to the Lake District. It has held a weekly market since the Middle Ages, and every Saturday stalls still set up around the Moot Hall in the centre of the town (now home to the tourist office). Keswick holds annual jazz and film festivals, during which the town is rather more crowded and buzzing, while its Theatre by the Lake (*see p138*) is the best performance venue in the area.

Cars of the Stars Motor Museum

Boys young and old, as well as film and television buffs, will be in their element at this museum dedicated to acquiring some of the most iconic cars that have graced our screens. The time-travelling car from *Back to the Future*, the loveable Volkwagen Beetle called Herbie, Batman's batmobile, the classic yet curious car called Chitty Chitty Bang Bang, Peter Sellers' Mini from the *Pink Panther* films, James Bond's various Aston Martins, even Del Boy's battered old Robin Reliant from the sitcom *Only Fools and Horses* are all on display here. In addition the museum hires out vehicles for special occasions – imagine turning up to your wedding in Mad Max's Interceptor, or arriving en masse at an event in the *A Team* van!

Standish Street. Tel: 01768 773757. www.carsofthestars.com. Open: Easter–

Nov daily 10am–5pm; Dec Sat–Sun 10am–5pm. Admission charge.

Cumberland Pencil Museum

The humble pencil was created in Cumbria, produced from graphite from the Seathwaite mine, which is recreated at the entrance to this museum. All manner of pencil manufacture is explored here, including the changing machinery that has been used down the centuries, as well as historic boxes of pencils that will send older visitors down memory lane. Also on display is the world's longest pencil, and the museum is particularly appealing for children with dedicated areas allowing them to draw and experiment with a variety of pencil products.
Southey Works. Tel: 01768 773626. www.pencilmuseum.co.uk. Open: daily 9.30am–5pm (last admission 4pm). Admission charge.

The Cumberland Pencil Museum in Keswick

Keswick Mining Museum

Mining has been an important factor in the area since the 16th century. By the 19th century, with the production of pencils and the advantage of rail travel to allow exportation, mining was the mainstay of the local economy. This museum uncovers all the factors about the geology of the area (including a prehistoric section), mining techniques through the ages and the often brutal and dangerous lives of the men who worked the pits.
Otley House, Otley Road. Tel: 01768 780055. www.keswickminingmuseum.co.uk. Open: Apr–Oct daily 10am–5pm; Nov–Mar Tue–Sun 10am–5pm. Admission charge.

Keswick Museum and Art Gallery

There's an eclectic mix of displays here: stuffed animals, antique bicycles, local geological finds and more. One area of the museum is dedicated to the Lake poets (*see pp44–5*) with priceless

The view from Brantwood, John Ruskin's home above Coniston Water

manuscripts, letters and other memorabilia belonging to Wordsworth

---

THE CONISTON UFO

One of the more bizarre tales associated with Coniston in the 20th century was the supposed sighting of a UFO above the peak of the Old Man of Coniston. A local 14-year-old boy claimed to have seen a saucer-like shape lighting up the sky in February 1954, in an era when curiosity and hysteria about UFOs seemed to be at its height. Photographs were apparently taken of the object but went missing, and the boy eventually confessed he'd made the whole thing up, but conspiracy theorists still ponder over the whole event.

---

and Robert Southey. The most famous exhibit, however, is the stone dulcimer, a sort of piano-cum-xylophone made of different stones that can, remarkably, be played in tune.
Station Road. Tel: 01768 773263.
Open: Apr–Oct Tue–Sat 10am–4pm.
Free admission.

Puzzling Place

It's all about optical illusions here – holograms, defying gravity, strange artworks all designed to deceive the naked eye. There's also a puzzle area that will have visitors scratching their

heads for hours trying to solve the various challenges. A great rainy day option.
Museum Square. Tel: 01768 775102 www.puzzlingplace.co.uk. Open: daily 10am–6pm. Free admission.

CONISTON

The name Coniston can be divided into two parts: the 8km (5-mile) long Coniston Water and Coniston village on its banks. Coniston Water is one of the most popular of the 'lakes', with leisurely cruises undertaken in summer (the speed limit for any boating craft is restricted to 16km/h (10mph), while a hike to the top of the famous Old Man of Coniston peak is a must-do for avid walkers. Two names most readily associated with Coniston are the writer John Ruskin and the speedboat racer Donald Campbell (*see pp38–9*), both of whom are buried in the village's St Andrew's Church.

Brantwood

Stunningly situated on the shores of Coniston Water, John Ruskin's one-time home is now a museum dedicated to displaying the art critic's valuable and wide-ranging personal collection of paintings, furniture and more. On a fine day, however, don't miss the opportunity to explore the eight gardens, all with different botanical themes, and the surrounding woodland. The house regularly stages special events too, from art courses to outdoor theatre.

JOHN RUSKIN

Poet, artist and critic, John Ruskin (1819–1900) was a prominent figure in literary circles during his lifetime. He was largely responsible, in his championing of his work as an art critic, for the reputation that Turner has to this day for his naturalistic landscapes, as well as the success of Pre-Raphaelites such as Rossetti and Millais (who was later to marry Ruskin's wife). He was also passionate about architecture, particularly the neo-Gothic style that was to emerge in the 19th century, was influential in the establishment of the National Trust, among other things, and in later life became devoted to socialist ideals.

Brantwood. Tel: 01539 441396. www.brantwood.org.uk. Open: mid-Mar–mid-Nov daily 11am–5.30pm. Admission charge.

Ruskin Museum

Despite its name, this museum is not solely dedicated to the writer but all aspects of life, history and people of Coniston. As well as articles that once belonged to Ruskin, there are exhibits about Donald Campbell, a boat that once belonged to Arthur Ransome of *Swallows and Amazons* fame (*see p41*), and areas devoted to local industry such as the copper mines that once made the area wealthy, and lace making and local agriculture, in particular Herdwick sheep.
Yewdale Road. Tel: 01539 441164. www.ruskinmuseum.com. Open: Mar–mid-Nov daily 10am–5.30pm; mid-Nov–Feb Wed–Sun 10.30am–3.30pm. Admission charge.

Donald Campbell and *Bluebird*

One of the most tragic yet inspiring human tales associated with the Lake District is that of Donald Campbell (1921–67), the car and boat racer who devoted his life to breaking speed records.

Racing was clearly in his genes from birth. His father, Sir Malcolm Campbell (1885–1948) made his name and earned himself a knighthood for racing and record-breaking in the 1920s and 30s, and Donald took up the family mantle in the 50s.

Naming his boats *Bluebird*, as his father had done before him, Campbell used the vast water expanses of the Lakes to practise and attempt water speed records, which he consistently achieved: 324km/h (202mph) in Ullswater in 1955 and six further speed increases culminating with 444km/h (276mph) in Australia in 1964. That same year he also broke the land speed record in the Bluebird CN7 car with a speed of 648km/h (403mph). These combined records remain unique by one person, but, of course, the very nature of record-breaking means that figures are always set to be broken, and Campbell was not content to rest on his laurels.

During the winter of 1966 he returned to the Lake District at Coniston Water (*see p37*) to attempt to better the water speed record in the *Bluebird K7*. The project was plagued by mechanical problems and bad weather, which should perhaps have been a warning to delay the continued efforts. Tragically on 4 January 1967, in his latest attempt, the *Bluebird* hit a patch of turbulent water at a speed of 510km/h (320mph), was thrust up high into the air, flipped over and nosedived back into the lake, breaking up and killing Campbell in the process. Only the faithful teddy that he carried with him

Donald Campbell, standing beside *Bluebird* in 1966

One of the *Bluebird*'s attempts on the water speed record on Coniston Water

as a mascot was found bobbing on the water – the *Bluebird* and Campbell's body could not be found. Sadder still, much of the event was captured on film by a man named John Lomax, who was fascinated by Campbell's career, but the film *Campbell at Coniston* does offer a lasting legacy of this courageous man.

Both the boat and the body were not to be recovered until 2001 when a diver named Bill Smith and his team went in search of the wreck using better location techniques that had developed over the ensuing decades. Campbell could finally be buried at St Andrew's Church in Coniston, in a blue coffin in memory of the name of his beloved vessel. There is also a memorial to Campbell in the town, and in the Ruskin Museum (*see p37*) are various items detailing the life of the man and his achievements. There is also an ongoing project to rebuild *Bluebird K7* and display it in a specially built wing of the museum.

WINDERMERE

The best known of all the lakes in the region, largely due to its size, stretching 17km (10.5 miles) in a long thin path from north to south, the area around Windermere is the hub of the tourist industry. There's not much to Windermere town itself, but all around are hikes, hills, boating opportunities and various historic sights that can keep visitors occupied for days. Within the lake are 18 islands, and there is plenty of opportunity for fishing for trout and char in its waters. Beware however – legend has it that a lake monster lurks within its 67m (220ft) depths.

Ambleside

At the northern end of Windermere is the town of Ambleside, a popular tourist hub. Its most famous building is Bridge House, a curious two-room edifice that seems to hover above the stream, supposedly built in this way to avoid land taxation. It now belongs to the National Trust. Also of note in the town is St Mary's Church, inside which is a large mural depicting the annual rushbearing ceremony (see p25).

Rydal Mount

Just outside Ambleside, this charming 16th-century house was home to William Wordsworth and various members of his family from 1813, and is in fact still in part lived in by his descendants. It was here that the poet wrote his greatest work *The Prelude* as well as many other acclaimed pieces. Wordsworth's study, from which he

Lake Windermere at Bowness-on-Windermere

composed his verse, can be visited, as can the living room with original furniture and some of the bedrooms. The terraced gardens remain much as they did when landscaped by Wordsworth during his time here. *Rydal. Tel: 01539 433002. www.rydalmount.co.uk. Open: Mar–Oct daily 9.30am–5pm; Nov–Feb Wed–Mon 10am–4pm. Admission charge.*

Blackwell

There are numerous beautiful mansions lining the banks of Windermere (many of which are now luxury hotels), but Blackwell has been preserved as a museum for its beautiful architecture and interior design. Built by architect Mackay Hugh Baillie Scott, it fully embraces the Arts and Craft movement that became popular at the turn of the 20th century. Inside there is beautiful oak panelling, a minstrel's gallery, vast stone fireplaces, a striking white living room and various other design details such as brightly coloured stained glass and blue-and-white Dutch Delft tiles. A must for anybody with an interest in art or design.

Bowness-on-Windermere. Tel: 01539 446139. www.blackwell.org.uk. Open: daily 10.30am–5pm. Admission charge.

Brockhole

The official visitors' centre for the Lake District National Park is housed in this beautiful house overlooking Windermere, where you'll find all the

SWALLOWS AND AMAZONS

There are certain books that capture the glories of childhood like few others – Arthur Ransome's *Swallows and Amazons* is one such series. Ransome (1884–1967), though born in Yorkshire, made his adult home in the Lake District and used it as the setting for the first few of his Swallows and Amazons series (subsequent books were set in East Anglia and Scotland). The books, the first of which was published in 1930, detail the exploits of children from two different families, the Walkers, who have a boat named *Swallow*, and the Blacketts, who have a boat named *Amazon*. During an idyllic summer holiday they camp out on an island in the Lakes, and their various adventures, from fishing to 'piracy', make up much of the plot. While the names of the locations, such as Wild Cat Island, are entirely fictional, it is generally considered that much of the landscape emulates Lake Windermere and Coniston Water. The books have remained at the forefront of children's literature for decades, and in 1974 were made in to a successful film.

information needed for a holiday in the area as well as interesting exhibitions. Another highlight here are the gardens that in spring come in to a glorious bloom of wild flowers.

Brockhole. Tel: 01539 446601. Open: Feb–Oct daily 10am–5pm. Free admission.

Townend

Agriculture has been at the heart of Cumbrian life for centuries, as attested by this wonderful 17th-century farmhouse. Although in the hands of the National Trust, the same family line, the Brownes, that have lived here

Peter Rabbit on show at the World of Beatrix Potter

Troutbeck. Tel: 01539 432628.
Open: Apr–Oct Wed–Sun 1–5pm.
Admission charge.

The World of Beatrix Potter

The whole of Cumbria seems to be Potter potty, and this is a wonderful place to bring children familiar with her tales. Every one of Potter's animal characters and their stories have been brought to life in a cleverly landscaped environment recreating Mr McGregor's garden, where Peter Rabbit gets up to so many of his tricks, and the kitchen where Mrs Tiggywinkle bustles around, and more. For older children there's also an area dedicated to the life and works of Potter herself.

Bowness-on-Windermere. Tel: 01539 488444. www.hop-skip-jump.com.
Open: daily 10am–4.30pm.
Admission charge.

for 400 years are still responsible for preserving it, including many original pieces of furniture, much of which was carved by the family themselves from local oak wood.

Grasmere's main street

CANON RAWNSLEY AND THE NATIONAL TRUST

Although born in Surrey, Canon Rawnsley (1851–1920) settled in the Lake District in 1877 and soon became enchanted by his new surroundings. As well as his religious activities he became passionate about the preservation of the area from the heavy development and industrialisation that was taking place elsewhere in the country. He formed first The Friends of the Lake District, a society that was intended to bring awareness to the beauty of the surroundings, as well as establishing many educational institutions including Keswick High School. In 1895, after many years of trying, he set up the National Trust, with two other keen conservationists, as a society that would be able to buy (or receive donations for) specific areas or buildings of cultural or natural significance – early purchases included Brandlehow Wood and the Castlerigg Stone Circle, a prehistoric site near Skiddaw. Rawnsley also had a considerable influence on Beatrix Potter (*see pp22–3*), who first met him as a teenager on a family holiday in the Lakes. While he was the first person to really show an interest in her work, Rawnsley's work led Potter in later life to be an avid conservationist. Although the National Trust was initially concerned with the Lake District, in the past century it has expanded to protect and preserve places throughout the country, many of which would undoubtedly have been destroyed without Rawnsley's foresight and determination.

Lake District National Park

GRASMERE

Visitors to Grasmere are invariably drawn here by its associations with William Wordsworth, who lived in the village for many years and who is buried, alongside his wife, sister and some of his children, in St Oswald's Church. Another draw, right next to the church, is the famous Sarah Nelson's Gingerbread Shop, a must for cake-lovers to sample this delicious local speciality.

Dove Cottage

At one time a pub called the Dove and Olive, William Wordsworth and his sister Dorothy (and, for a period, Samuel Taylor Coleridge) lived in this converted cottage from 1799 to 1808. Many of their personal possessions can still be seen here, from furniture to other memorabilia, such as Wordsworth's ice skating boots. The house is unusual in that the bedrooms

are on the ground floor, while the upstairs room was used as a living room due to its sunnier disposition and views of the lake beyond (now, sadly, obscured by development). Much of our knowledge of their life at Dove

(*Cont. on p46*)

Inside Sarah Nelson's Gingerbread shop in Grasmere

The Lake Poets

The Lake District has a fairly strong literary heritage (*see pp4–5*), but two names most closely associated with the area in this respect are two masters of English literature, William Wordsworth and Samuel Taylor Coleridge.

Wordsworth (1770–1850) was a native Cumbrian, born in Cockermouth (*see pp32–4*); Coleridge (1772–1834) was born in Devon. But the two men met in 1795 and became steady friends. Wordsworth had already published some early poetry but it was the collaboration of the two in 1798 that produced the first of their famous *Lyrical Ballads* collections, which gave rise to the Romantic movement – a celebration of nature, emotion and beauty that was in part a backlash from the ugliness and practicalities of the Industrial Revolution. Within the collection were two of the poets' most famous works: *Tintern Abbey* by Wordsworth and *The Rime of the Ancient Mariner* by Coleridge. There were also some contributions from Wordsworth's sister Dorothy.

In 1799 Wordsworth and his sister moved into Dove Cottage in Grasmere (*see pp43 & 46*) where William worked on his most famous poem, the autobiographical *The Prelude* (which would eventually be

Dove Cottage, where Wordsworth worked on his most famous poems

published posthumously), as well as many other renowned pieces, including *I Wandered Lonely as a Cloud*. The following year Coleridge returned to England from Germany where he had worked on, among other things, translating the poems of Friedrich Schiller, and moved to Keswick, ostensibly to be near his co-writer friend. However, Coleridge was soon to become a serious opium (or laudanum) addict, which increasingly caused tensions between the two men, and Wordsworth broke off contact by 1810 (they would, however, resume their friendship in 1828). Coleridge eventually died in London where he had been trying to receive treatment for his addiction.

The Wordsworth family graves in St Oswald's churchyard in Grasmere

While not all his work was critically acclaimed during his lifetime Wordsworth did become Poet Laureate in 1843. He is buried in St Oswald's Church in Grasmere. Aside from the *Ancient Mariner* Coleridge's other great works are the opium-inspired strangeness of *Kubla Khan* and the Gothic poem *Christabel*, which was to inspire other writers of the age including Coleridge's friend Mary Shelley, author of *Frankenstein*. He is buried in St Michael's Church in Highgate, London.

The third poet who comes under the umbrella term the ' Lake Poets' is the now lesser-known Robert Southey (1774–1843), although he was highly respected in literary circles in his day. Born in Bristol, he met Coleridge while they were both students and gained a mutual admiration when they came up with the rather pie-in-the-sky idea of setting up a commune society in America, called pantisocracy. It came to nothing, but the two men remained close, a fact enhanced when they married two sisters, although Coleridge's union was not to last. Southey also moved to Keswick, where he continued to write poems and biographies of, among others, John Bunyan and Horatio Nelson, and was appointed Poet Laureate in 1813. Southey's best-known work is *The Inchcape Rock* and a short fairy story entitled *The Three Bears* which eventually became known as the Goldilocks story, when the concept was taken up by many subsequent writers. He is buried in St Kentigern's Church in Keswick.

Cottage comes from the detailed diary that Dorothy kept, known as the *Grasmere Journals*, and it was clearly a happy period for the poet – not only did he marry during his time here but his first three children were born here. On Wordsworth's departure the lease was taken up by their friend Thomas de Quincey, who would make his name with his work *The Confessions of an English Opium Eater*. The house is now in the hands of the Wordsworth Trust and next door to the cottage they run a museum that explores all aspects of the Romantic period, from poetry, to prose, to visual art.

A591, Grasmere. Tel: 01539 435544. www.wordsworth.org.uk. Open: daily 9.30am–5.30pm. Closed: Jan. Admission charge.

Heaton Cooper Studio

Alfred Heaton Cooper was a landscape artist who delighted in turning his Lakeland area into watercolours, and his son, William Heaton Cooper established this popular gallery in 1939 to display both his and his father's work. All successive generations of the family have since made their living in various art forms, so this truly is a family concern. In addition, there is a

A fine day at Derwentwater

A motor launch and rowing boats on Derwentwater

shop here selling high quality art projects if any visitors have gained inspiration and want to take to the canvas themselves.

The Studio. Tel: 01539 435280.
www.heatoncooper.co.uk.
Open: Mon–Sat 9am–5pm.
Free admission.

DERWENTWATER

Derwentwater is one of the most popular lakes for messing about in boats, in part due to is navigable size at just 5km (3 miles) in length. If you don't have your own boat or want to put in the work in a hired one, on a fine day there are few more relaxing things to do than take a trip on one of the many motor launches that operate here in summer and visit four of the islands in the lake, including Derwent Island, which boasts a folly of a fortress (never used for military purposes but just the creation of a 19th-century eccentric). St Herbert's island was a one-time pilgrimage site, and monks would sail to it from Friars Crag, a promontory that now offers some of the best views of the lake. Also at Friars Crag is a slate memorial to the writer John Ruskin (*see p37*) with a quote in his own words about the area, which now belongs to the National Trust.

Drive: Whinlatter and Bassenthwaite

A pleasant day of both driving and short easy walks that give a taster of more experienced hikes as well as the views on offer in this rambler's paradise, plus the chance to see some local wildlife.

Distance 25 miles. Allow a full day to take in all the attractions en route.

From Keswick (see pp34–7) drive 5km (3 miles) westwards out of town to Braithwaite.

1 Grisedale Pike

Park the car in Braithwaite village car park for the approximately one and a half hour walk to the top of this hill (the path is signposted) to take in views of Derwentwater, Bassenthwaite and Crummock Water.
Return to the car and continue out of Braithwaite along the B5292, known as the Whinlatter Pass, until you see signs for Whinlatter Forest Park.

2 Whinlatter Forest Park

This protected forest area is home to badgers and ospreys, among other wildlife, and there are numerous paths that allow you to explore the forest landscape. Maps are available at the visitor centre, which also has excellent exhibitions on the preservation of the forest and the people who work there, as well as detailed nature explanations.

Return to the A66 and follow the signs for Cockermouth.

3 Bassenthwaite Lake

It may sound bizarre but, strictly speaking, Bassenthwaite is the only

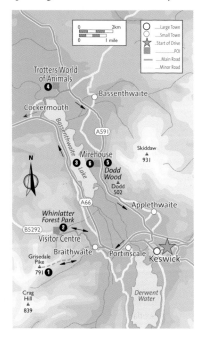

'real' lake in the Lake District – the others are either 'waters' or 'meres' (which means lake). It's a far more peaceful area than some of its larger counterparts because it is without all the motor launches that draw the crowds at places such as Windermere. It's a perennially popular spot for bird-watchers.

Continue north on the A66 to the northern edge of the lake, then turn right over the Ouse Bridge and follow the signs for Trotters World of Animals.

4 Trotters World of Animals

Perfect for families, this is part zoo, part conservation project, with animals such as bear, zebra and lynx, as well as plenty of hands-on activities and hawk-flying demonstrations (*see p151*).

Exit Trotters and take a left, joining the A591 southwards towards Keswick, parking in the car park of the Old Sawmill Tearooms.

5 Dodd Wood

The highlight of any visit to this woodland is the viewing platform that allows you to see nesting ospreys in their own habitat from April to August (after which they migrate for the winter to warmer climes). There are also marked walking trails within the wood.

6 Mirehouse

Next to Dodd Wood is this wonderful 17th-century house. The ground floor is open to the public, with its wonderful display of antique furniture, artworks, and letters to the one-time owner James Spedding by such notables as Alfred, Lord Tennyson. To add to the homely atmosphere, a pianist plays classical music as visitors stroll through the rooms.

Tel: 01768 772287. www.mirehouse.com. House. Open: Easter–Oct Wed & Sun 2–5pm. Gardens. Open: Mar–Nov daily 10.30am–5.30pm. Admission charge. Continue along the A591 back to Keswick.

Drive: Whinlatter and Bassenthwaite

The hills of Scotland can be seen in the distance over Bassenthwaite

NEAR SAWREY

This tiny little village would attract virtually no attention, despite its prettiness, if it wasn't for its one-time most famous resident Beatrix Potter, who, over her career, bought much land and property around the area.

Hill Top

As the success of her books began to increase, Beatrix Potter bought this 17th-century farmhouse in 1905 and, although she moved to a larger nearby house after she married in 1913, it is the place most readily associated with the author. Many of the illustrations in her charming children's tales about squirrels, rabbits, hedgehogs and more were influenced both by the farm's outside grounds and the interior décor of the cottage because this was the period when most of the stories were created. One of the most delightful aspects of a visit here is that Potter left the house to the National Trust on the strict understanding that it be preserved exactly as she had left it, and in that sense it almost feels like the writer is 'still there', with all her furniture and writing and painting equipment still to be seen.
Hilltop. Tel: 01539 436269.
Open: Mar–Oct Mon–Thur,
Sat & Sun 10.30am–4.30pm.
Admission charge.

GRANGE AND BORROWDALE

This area of woodland at the southern end of Derwentwater is renowned for its natural beauty, eulogised by the likes of Wordsworth and others.

Bowder Stone

Borrowdale is known for its random rocks strewn over the landscape and this 2,000-tonne sample, perilously tilted, is its most famous. Its origins are unknown but many geologists believe it journeyed here in the water flows from Scotland, after the Ice Age. Today a permanent ladder allows access to the top. Behind the stone is King's How, named after King Edward VII and one of the first purchases by the National Trust by its then president, Princess Louise, the king's sister. It's a popular area among walkers and birdwatchers.

Honister Slate Mine

The mining industry was sadly decimated during the 1980s in Britain, but this is the last actively working slate mine in England, excavating the beautiful Honister green slate that has been in use in building construction since the Middle Ages and perhaps earlier. If you're happy with confined spaces, a guided underground mine tour through the tunnels and caves to learn about the mining industry past and present is a memorable experience. Warm and waterproof clothes and footwear are recommended. Thrill seekers will also want to take the Via Ferrata trip – scrambling and climbing over the rocks and over the mine, attached to

The Bowder Stone in Borrowdale

a cable with a harness. The route follows a narrow gauge railway line that was constructed along the 305m (1,000ft) Honister Crag to transport the slate to level ground. If you're looking to decorate your patio or some other area, don't miss the 'Fill Ya Boot' service – the chance to fill your entire car boot with green slate for as little as £10.

Tel: 01768 777230. www.honister-slate-mine.co.uk. Open: Mon–Fri 9am–5pm, Sat & Sun 10am–5pm, mine tours 10.30am, 12.30pm, 3.30pm. Admission charge.

SCAFELL PIKE

Only experienced climbers should attempt the ascent to the top of the 978m (3,209ft) Scafell Pike – England's highest mountain – but once there, the views are truly spectacular. Combined with Ben Nevis in Scotland and Snowdon in Wales it forms part of the Three Peaks Challenge, which is attempted by mountaineers every year. The most popular (and therefore most crowded) route is from Wasdale Head, but there is also the Corridor Route from Seathwaite, which requires a good deal more stamina and expertise.

Woodland in Borrowdale

Scafell Pike in winter, taken from the summit of Coniston Old Man

Obviously all the safety rules apply (*see p149*) for anyone attempting the mountain, and around six hours should be allowed for a full ascent and descent.

BUTTERMERE

Surrounded as it is by fells, as well as the boating activities available on its lake and neighbouring Crummock Water, this is a popular destination in summer but still without the full-on tourist activity that can be found at Coniston and Windermere. The beauty of the area was one of the great loves of Alfred Wainwright's life and it's no coincidence that his ashes were

scattered here – a plaque in the village church is dedicated to his memory. Buttermere is also famous for the 'maid of Buttermere'. In the late 18th century a local pub landlord's daughter was renowned for her beauty and caught the eye of a so-called Colonel Hope, who married her with much fanfare. After the marriage, however, it was revealed that Hope was not only already married to someone else but also no colonel at all – just a plain-sounding man named John Hatfield. He was hanged in Carlisle in 1803 and poor Mary returned to Buttermere, forged an altogether more humble marriage to a farmer and attempted to disassociate herself from the scandal. The tale was made even more popular by the author and television broadcaster Melvyn Bragg's novel on the subject (*see p20*).

HAWKSHEAD

There are a surprising number of attractions in Hawkshead given the small size of the village and, of course, Beatrix Potter rears her head yet again with her associations with the place. Wordsworth, too, that other great fixture of the Lake District, has plenty of connections with the village.

Beatrix Potter Gallery

Not far from Near Sawrey and set in the solicitor's office that was used by Potter's husband, William Heelis, there are wonderful displays of Potter's

ALFRED WAINWRIGHT

Few people have done more to promote the beauty and walking pleasures of the Lake District than the writer and illustrator Alfred Wainwright (1907–91). Lancastrian by birth, he first visited the Lakes in 1930 and fell in love with the area so deeply that he relocated to Kendal for the rest of his life. An avid walker, Wainwright began to jot down words and pictures detailing his hikes in the early 1950s and these eventually turned into the *Pictorial Guide to the Lakeland Fells*, seven volumes documenting the area that remain as popular today as they were when they were back then, although they are currently undergoing slight revisions for the first time in their history. Wainwright also devised the famous Coast to Coast Walk, a 305km (190-mile) route taking in Cumbria and North Yorkshire. So influential was he to the area that the 214 fells that he documented are now affectionately known as 'the Wainwrights'. After his death, Wainwright's ashes were scattered on Haystacks, his favourite fell in the Buttermere Valley, according to his wishes.

A view over Hawkshead village

The Hawkshead Grammar School Museum

original artworks. There's also a more recent exhibition about the filming of Miss Potter, including how locations were chosen and recreated.
Main Street, Hawkshead.
Tel: 01539 436187. Open: Mar–Oct Mon–Thur, Sat & Sun 10.30am–4.30pm. Admission charge.

Hawkshead Grammar School

Established in 1585, within a comparatively short time the school in this small village had the unlikely reputation for being one of the best in the country, teaching its pupils Latin, ancient Greek, arithmetic and science. Among its past alumni is, of course, William Wordsworth who not only wrote a poem about the school but fulfilled that time-honoured schoolboy stunt of carving his name on to his wooden desk, which can still be seen. The school closed in 1909 and today is a charming museum, exploring the history of education through the ages and preserving the original furniture of both pupils and masters.
Rydal Road. Tel: 01539 436735. www.hawksheadgrammar.org.uk. Open: Apr–Sept Mon–Sat 10am–1pm, 2–5pm, Sun 1–5pm; Oct Mon–Sat 10am–1pm, 2–3.30pm, Sun 1–3.30pm. Free admission.

North Cumbria

North Cumbria was an important site for the Romans, who undertook their monumental project of Hadrian's Wall here. The region got caught up in the battles between the Scots and the English (from which many of the surviving pele towers date) and then with the lawlessness of the border reivers. Today it's a peaceful agricultural area, with rolling farmland grazed by sheep and cattle that contribute so much to the local economy.

CARLISLE

At the centre of North Cumbria is the county's capital, Carlisle, which boasts a range of historical buildings and fine museums, as well as plenty of accommodation (*see pp163–5*) and shopping options (*see p142*).

Carlisle to Settle Railway

One of the most picturesque railway experiences in Britain is the 116km (72-mile) long train journey from Carlisle journeying south to Settle in Yorkshire. The line was constructed in 1876 as some 6,000 brave engineers

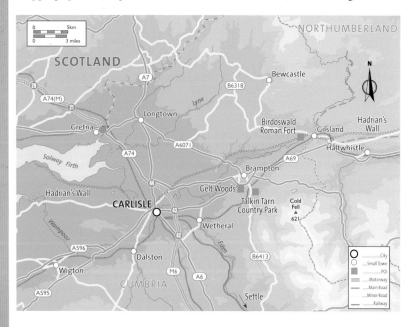

Carlisle Castle dates back to the 12th century

blasted 14 tunnels through the mountainous landscape and constructed over 20 viaducts to complete the route. This was dangerous work and many died during the seven-year construction process (some due to a smallpox epidemic that raged at the time rather than through injury), and memorials to those men can still be seen en route.

Unlike many of the railway lines in the area, which were constructed to carry mining and other industrial goods, the Carlisle to Settle line was ostensibly a passenger service and it greatly enhanced the tourist industry to both the Lake District and Scotland. With the advancement of higher speed trains, however, the line was threatened with closure in the 1980s, given the deterioration in its facilities. However, conservationists petitioned heartily against the move, and in 1989 British Rail agreed to keep the line open and in good repair. The trains are generally diesel these days, but there are occasional steam train journeys, which are a must for any railway buff. Highlights along the route include the original Victorian stations (some renovated but in keeping with the original style), the visitors' centre at Ribblesdale and the chance to look around the original signal box at Settle. For details of timetables and fares, visit *www.settle-carlisle.co.uk*

Walk: Carlisle

As administrative capital of the county of Cumbria, Carlisle is its most important city. First settled by the Romans, it was later at the forefront of the battles between the Scots, the English and the border reivers (see pp66–7) until the creation of a unified Britain in the 17th century.

The walk covers approximately 3.5km (2¼ miles) and takes around three hours.

Start from Carlisle Railway Station.

1 Citadel

The two large towers that can be seen opposite the railway station were the original gateways to the city.
Turn left on to English Street and continue to the corner of Castle Street and St Mary's Gate.

2 Carlisle Cathedral

Dating from the early 12th century, Carlisle's cathedral is one of the finest in northern England. There are a number of features of note here: the painted ceiling that details the life of St Cuthbert and the Apostles; St Wilfred's Chapel with its 16th-century altar; beautiful stained glass that has been preserved and added to over the centuries; and various examples of wood carving. There's also a treasury with a range of gold and silver religious items covering the period of the cathedral's history.
The Abbey. Tel: 01228 548151.
www.carlislecathedral.org.uk.

Open: Mon–Sat 7.40am–6.15pm, Sun 7.40am–5pm. Admission free but donations appreciated.
From The Abbey, turn left on to Castle Street.

3 Tullie House Museum

Probably the finest museum in Cumbria, this eclectic collection covers archaeology and fine arts, including a fantastic collection of Pre-Raphaelite works, as well as local quilting techniques.
Castle Street. Tel: 01228 618718.
www.tulliehouse.co.uk. Open: Apr–June & Sept–Oct Mon–Sat 10am–5pm, Sun 12–5pm; July–Aug Mon–Sat 10am–5pm, Sun 11am–5pm. Admission charge.
Continue up Castle Street and turn left on to Annetwell Street, taking the pedestrian bridge over Castle Way to the castle.

4 Carlisle Castle

Given its position on the border between England and Scotland, Carlisle Castle has played a very important role

in the skirmishes between the two countries over the centuries. Originally dating from the 12th century, but modified several times during its history, this was not only a vital defensive structure but also a prison: Mary, Queen of Scots was held captive here in 1568.
Castle Street. Tel: 01228 625600. www.carlislecastle.com. Open: Apr–Sept daily 9.30am–5pm; Oct–Mar daily 10am–4pm. Admission charge.
Take the pedestrian underpass under Castle Way and continue down West Tower Street and right on to Market Street.

5 Market Hall

Renovated in 1990, this lovely 19th-century market place remains one of Carlisle's main shopping areas, all housed under a glass roof and with elaborate ironwork and other Victorian details.
At the end of Market Street, turn left on to Fisher Street.

6 Guildhall Museum

Many craftsmen and tradesmen in the Middle Ages had to belong to a guild in order to market their wares, and this 15th-century building was their meeting house. Today it houses a museum dedicated to their activities as well as to a history of Carlisle and Cumbria in general.
Green Market. Tel: 01228 618718. Open: Apr–Oct daily 12–4.30pm. Admission charge.

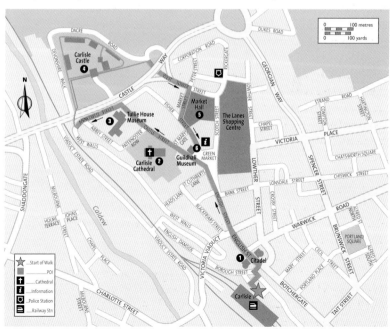

Walk: Carlisle

HADRIAN'S WALL

When the Romans originally invaded Britain (*see pp16–17*) their plan would have been to occupy the entire land, but as the years progressed it became increasingly apparent that the Picts in Scotland were a greater force to be reckoned with than had been anticipated. When the Emperor Hadrian came to England in AD 122 there were troubled times in the English faction of the empire and he decided to construct a wall to define the borders between Roman-occupied England and the tribal lands further north. Originally 117km (73 miles) in length, stretching from Ravenglass in southern Cumbria (*see pp104–7*), all the way along the north border and across to the River Tyne on the east coast of the country, Hadrian's Wall was a staggering feat of engineering, man power and sheer determination that took a total of six years to complete. What is equally remarkable today is that, while the wall is in no way existent in its entirety, so much of it still stands as a testament to Roman Britain. A walk along its route takes you past even more Roman gems, including several Roman forts that were put in place to defend the wall and the frontier line that it signified.

The wall was built by the 2nd, 6th and 20th Roman legions who occupied northern England at the time, who excavated local limestone for the project, bonded together with local clay. As well as forts, there were also several turrets that were built as lookout points to warn of possible invasions. A deep ditch on either side of the wall was also a further defensive measure.

Hadrian's Wall can be followed on foot for much of its length

Birdoswald is one of the best-preserved forts along Hadrian's Wall

There were still ambitions to take over the land north of the border, and the next Roman emperor in Britain built the Antonine Wall in the Border region. But they were still flummoxed by the inhospitality and warring skills of the Scots, and the latter wall was abandoned and Hadrian's Wall re-manned in AD 164.

Although it remained a feature of the northern English landscape over the ensuing centuries, the desire to preserve history was not a popular concept until the 19th century. By then, large stretches of the wall had been dismantled in order to build newer buildings with the stone. It was a local lawyer by the name of John Clayton who took it upon himself to buy land in the area in the mid-19th century, in an effort to preserve what was left of the wall. It is Clayton, and later the National Trust, whom we can

thank for what remains of it today. Now designated a UNESCO World Heritage Site, there is a national walking trail (summer only) as well as cycle paths and bus routes that allow visitors to see this astonishing historic monument for themselves.
www.hadrians-wall.org

Birdoswald Roman Fort

Probably the best place to get a full idea of the enormity of Hadrian's project is at this former Roman fort where some of the original building can still be seen, including the turret. In the visitors' centre there is a model of both the original fort as archaeologists believe it to have looked, as well as the entire length of the wall.
Gilsand. Tel: 01697 747602.
Open: Apr–Sept daily 10am–5.30pm;
Oct daily 10am–4pm. Admission charge.

The Kingdom of Rheged

Following the departure of the Romans from Britain (*see pp16–17*), much of what is now Cumbria (and parts of Yorkshire, Northumbria and Strathclyde, over the Scottish border) became a kingdom known as Rheged, with its main base thought to be around what is now Carlisle. It was ruled over by the Brythonic (British) king Urien in the 6th century, one of the legendary figures of early British history. He and his people were Christian Celts who spoke a language known as Cumbric and in large part

Owain appeals to King Arthur, an illustration by Walter Crane in *King Arthur's Knight* by Henry Gilbert

hailed from what is now the country of Wales. In fact, the Welsh connection is still clearly apparent today in the county's name – Cumbria (and formerly Cumberland) take their etymology from the Welsh name for their own nation, Cymru.

Urien had a distinguished heritage, following on from the lineage of a great military leader Coel Hen (more popularly known through the children's nursery rhyme as Old King Cole). A fine warrior himself, Urien was for a long time successful in battling and defeating the Saxons (or Angles), who were attempting to occupy Britain from their base on the island of Lindisfarne off the east coast and a region known as Bernicia, which is modern-day Northumbria. By all accounts Urien was an impressive military force, and after a number of battles over the years had almost entirely seen off the Saxon threat. However, in around AD 590 he was betrayed by his former ally Morcant, who ordered Urien's assassination by beheading in an ambitious drive to take over as leader. He was, in fact, succeeded by his son Owain but, despite concerted efforts, Owain was never able to command battles with the same skill as his father and was

The Eden Valley near Carlisle, said to be the heartland of Rheged

killed only a few years later. He is said to be buried in St Andrew's Church in Penrith, but like so many of these tales, this could just be pure romanticism or speculation.

Urien and his son Owain remain popular figureheads as the last of the great Celts, in both Welsh literature (notably in medieval texts known as the *Welsh Triads*) and in the ever-popular Arthurian tales. In the latter, Urien of Gore, as he is then known, marries Morgan le Fay, Arthur's sister, and Owain (Ywain), although initially at odds with the legendary 'High-King', was eventually to become one of the Knights of the Round Table. Their names also appear in works by Geoffrey Chaucer, Chrétien de Troyes, Malory and Alfred, Lord Tennyson, all of whom were recreating the myths and legends of this time. But perhaps the greatest indicator of how important Urien was in his own lifetime is that he had his own poet travelling with him, Taleisin, from whose writings we gain much of the history of the man and his time in the *Book of Taleisin*.

The kingdom of Rheged was eventually and perhaps inevitably taken by the more powerful Saxons, and the Cumbric language and much of the Celtic culture and traditions disappeared for good.

North Cumbria

DALSTON

The most notable building in Dalston is **Dalston Hall**, architecturally important because of its early 16th-century pele tower, although the rest of the building comprises additions made in the 17th, 18th and 19th centuries. The hall now functions as a hotel. Another far older pele tower (1340) can be seen at the nearby **Rose Castle**, which is home to the Bishop of Carlisle. The building was badly damaged during the ravages of the English Civil War and was largely renovated in the 17th and 18th centuries.

Dalston Hall: Dalston.
Tel: 01228 710271.
www.dalston-hall.co.uk.
Rose Castle: Closed to the public.

BRAMPTON

The centre of the small market town of Brampton is dominated by **Moot Hall**, an octagonal building that is now home to the tourist office but was once the scene of a weekly poultry market. Another important building is **St Martin's Church**, which is notable for its beautiful stained-glass windows, created by Pre-Raphaelite artist Sir Edward Burne-Jones in the workshop of William Morris. These dazzling, colourful works depicting Biblical scenes, the life of St Martin, and a wonderful pelican image, turn an otherwise rather functional looking construction into something quite unexpected.

St Martin's Church: Font Street.
Open: 9.30am–4.30pm.

Dalston Hall incorporates a 16th-century pele tower

St Martin's Church in Brampton dates from 1878

Just outside Brampton is the **Talkin Tarn Country Park** with its lakes and parks ideal for watersports, fishing, cycling or simply strolling in the woodland. Also just outside is **Gelt Woods**, where a large quarry that was used by the Romans to excavate stone for Hadrian's Wall can still be seen.

LONGTOWN

Situated as it is, just a couple of miles from the Scottish border, Longtown has inevitably had a long history of battles between the two countries until peace was finally restored in the 17th century. Just outside the town was one of the most famous battles, the Battle of Solway Moss in 1542. Furious at a recent English invasion, King James V of Scotland organised an army of around 15,000 men and marched south over the border, but their plans were disorganised and confused. An English army of just 3,000 met them at Solway Moss and defeated them with ease. It

was one loss too many for James, who would be dead within a fortnight of the battle, his throne being ascended by his six-year-old daughter Mary, Queen of Scots – and another half century of trouble would ensue. Today Longtown is best known for its large sheep and cattle markets.

BEWCASTLE

Bewcastle came into significance during the Roman period when a fort was established here as part of the defences of Hadrian's Wall. Today it is best known for its 7th-century Anglican cross in the grounds of St Cuthbert's Church, its 14m (46ft) height carved with figures of saints, runic inscriptions and an ancient sundial.

Also in Bewcastle are the remains of a 3rd century AD hexagonal Roman fort that would once have been home to a 1,000-strong protective force and was dedicated to the god Cocidius.

Border reivers

*'Oh were there war between the
    lands,
As well I wot there is none,
I would slight Carlisle castell high,
Though it were builded of marble
    stone.*

*I would set that castell in a lowe,
And sloken it with English blood;
There's nevir a man in Cumberland
Should ken where Carlisle castell
    stood.'*

This is just part of the long *Ballad of
Kinmont Willie* telling the tale of a
Scottish border reiver (thief) arrested
and imprisoned in Carlisle Castle
during the bloody period in history
that saw lawlessness run amok along
the borders between England and
Scotland.

Until the Union of the Crowns in
1603, when James VI of Scotland also
became James I of England, the
battles between England and
Scotland, for the former to gain
control of the latter, had occurred
regularly. During the latter part of the
16th century, however, war between
the two countries had abated, largely
due to the fact that Elizabeth I and
Mary, Queen of Scots both had such
tenuous control over their crowns that
their focus was directed away from a
region that had for centuries been the
scene of so many battles and
skirmishes. Thus an anarchic culture
prevailed, with little intervention by
the rulers of either nation.

The border between England and
Scotland was officially designated in
the Treaty of York in 1237 and the
lands on either side were known as
'marches', which were overseen by
wardens, ostensibly to keep order in
what were always troublesome
places. There were three marches on
the east side of the border – the West
March in England covers the region
around Carlisle that is now Cumbria,
and was probably the most important
because of its vulnerable geographical
position. There was also a 32km (20-
mile) stretch known as the Debatable
Land, which did not officially belong
to either country. During the majority
of the 16th century, but culminating
in the final two decades, these areas
fell prey to disorder and chaos of
massive proportions.

The main players in these events
were the border reivers. They were
made up of clan-like families (known
as 'riding surnames'), who lived on the
borders between the two countries
and developed a gang-like culture;

raiding, pillaging and destroying rival lands and property in their wake. They operated on horseback and wore steel-enhanced vests, round metal helmets and carried weaponry in the form of either swords, axes or crossbows. Their main spoils were livestock taken from rival families, but they generally stole whatever was available to them. As the mayhem continued, this was not so much a 'war' between England and Scotland – these people considered themselves 'border people' first and foremost – but pure and simple anarchy at a time when law and order was all but absent. Indeed there was often co-operation between the two countries if it meant attacking a mutual enemy.

The region was brought back under control with the reign of King James I, and the reivers were either arrested and imprisoned or reformed themselves into respectable land owners.

As with so much of history, particularly where it involves crime and misdemeanours, much of the activities of the reivers has transformed into myth and legend, so a certain amount of exaggeration can be assumed. But they were certainly a dominant force on that part of the landscape for many years. From them there are several words that still remain commonplace in the English language such as gang, kidnap and blackmail.

Arnside Tower is a 15th-century pele tower near the Lancashire border

East Cumbria

East Cumbria, on the border with Northumberland and North Yorkshire, is the least toured area of the county, but that's not to say there isn't plenty to see and do. Probably the most picturesque and popular area is along the River Eden, which flows from the Yorkshire border all the way across to the Solway Forth and out into the Irish Sea.

Penrith is the largest town in the area, but the highlights are the many small villages that dot the region, which are strewn with pretty farmers' cottages and old-fashioned inns and pubs. Steam railways, castle ruins and historic houses all add to the mix, so it is well worth leaving behind the crowds within the national park proper to explore this small pocket of England.

PENRITH

Although Carlisle (*see pp56–9*) is the county capital, Penrith is truly the main town of the Lake District proper, benefiting as it does from access by both motorway and rail. As a town in its own right, it's fairly generic, with most of the high street stores lining its pavements those that can be seen in any other major town in Britain, but there are several places of interest within its vicinity.

Dalemain Historic House

There has been a family residence here since the Middle Ages, and while it remains a private family home, the present owners have now opened many of the rooms, such as the Georgian panelled drawing room, to the public in order to share the glories of its architectural heritage. In fact the house is a bit of a treasure chest of English history – the Georgian façade, for example, leads on to the original 16th-century courtyard, while the pele tower (*see pp102–3*) is the original, dating from Norman times. Other highlights include artworks, antique furniture and a wonderful array of historical toys in the nursery. In the grounds there is also a beautiful rose garden, a traditional Tudor garden and agricultural relics in the barn.

Dalemain, Penrith.
Tel: 01768 486450.
www.dalemain.com.
House. Open: Apr–Oct Sun–Thur 11.15am–4pm.
Gardens. Open: Apr–Oct Sun–Thur 10am–5pm. Admission charge.

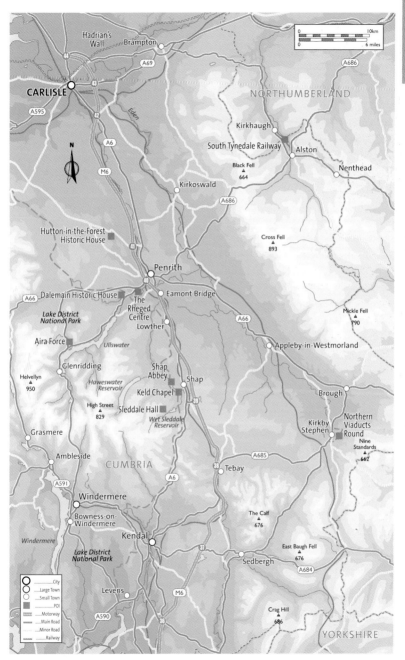

Hutton-in-the-Forest Historic House

Another private mansion that has been opened to the public by its owners, also originating with a 14th-century pele tower and altered and renovated over the centuries, including the elaborate Renaissance-style east front and the turreted and impressive 19th-century south front. Highlights inside include a wonderfully carved staircase, original William Morris wallpaper in the drawing room and bedroom and a striking oak-panelled hallway. The gardens are also a delight, with ponds, a woodland area, rhododendron bushes, topiary and various wildflowers.
Hutton-in-the-Forest, Penrith.
Tel: 01768 484449.
www.hutton-in-the-forest.co.uk.
House. Open: May–Sept Wed–Thur &
Sun 12.30–4pm.
Gardens. Open: Apr–Oct Sun–Fri
11am–5pm. Admission charge.

Penrith Castle

Sadly now in ruins, Penrith Castle was an important defensive post in the 15th century, when raids from Scotland were a common occurrence, and it was once occupied by King Richard III.
Castle Park. No telephone. Open: daily.
Free admission.

Penrith Museum

Housed in a former schoolhouse, originally built in 1670, this is the place to come if you want to learn more about Penrith and the surrounding Eden Valley. The main focus of the collection is archaeological finds from the surrounding area, primarily from the Bronze Age, but there is a regular programme of changing exhibitions that take a particular local topic and explore it in more depth. The building is also home to the tourist information centre so is a valuable source of what's going on in the town and the area.
Middlegate. Tel: 01768 817817.
Open: Mon–Sat 10am–5pm.
Free admission.

The Rheged Centre

Britain's largest grass-roofed building may be a rather strange claim to fame, but the Rheged Centre is now a hugely successful exhibition and entertainment venue for the Lake District. There is a permanent exhibition here entitled 'Discovering Cumbria', which offers all the information about the county over the centuries from its Celtic heritage to the present day. There is also a regular programme of touring exhibitions and trade shows. On site there is also a giant cinema screen that brings epic documentaries about the world's landscape, past and present, to life, and a number of shops and eateries for a bit of retail and refreshment therapy.
Redhills. Tel: 01768 868000.
www.rheghed.com.
Open: daily 10am–5.30pm.
Free admission.

The ruins of 15th-century Penrith Castle

Drive: Around Eamont Bridge

Cumbria was once divided into two counties – Cumberland and Westmorland – the boundaries of which were at the Eamont River. This small region is rich in historical interest, covering periods from prehistoric times to the 17th century, and makes for a pleasant half-day's drive. All the sights are open daily and have free admission.

Distance: 8km (5 miles).

Start the drive in Eamont Bridge, which is famous for its humped river crossing from which the village takes its name.

1 Eamont Bridge

The construction of the M6 motorway that now runs parallel to the village means that locals no longer have the traffic congestion they once did, but for the first half of the 20th century horns would beep in frustration trying to navigate this narrow crossing.
Leave Eamont Bridge to the east and follow the B6262 to Brougham.

2 Brougham Hall

Another ancestral home that is partly in ruins is currently being restored to preserve its wonderful turreted architecture. At present there is a craft workshop on site, with plans to include further attractions.
Turn right on to the B6262 and follow the signs to the A66. Brougham Castle is on the left.

3 Brougham Castle

The ruins of this 13th-century castle (built on the site of a former Roman fort) was last lived in during the 17th century by Lady Anne Clifford,

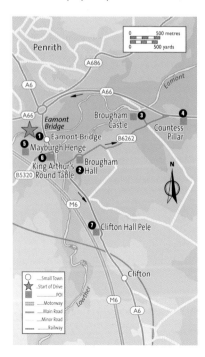

a local landowner who built or restored a number of properties in Cumbria and Yorkshire. A 160km (100-mile) public trail is now dedicated to her memory, taking in many of the places connected with her. Today a few of the rooms as well as the original keep can still be seen and it makes for a romantic stroll amid the decaying walls nestling on the riverbank.
Return to the B6262, turn left, then right on to the A66.

4 Countess Pillar

At the point that the road from Brougham meets the A66 there is a decorated pillar within a gated enclosure, erected by Lady Anne Clifford in dedication to her mother at the precise spot where Anne last saw her. As well as an inscription honouring her mother, the pillar also acts as a sundial.
Take the A66 towards Penrith and turn left at the roundabout, then first right on to the B5320.

5 Mayburgh Henge

The origins of this strip of land are unclear but the monolith that still stands here indicates that it may well once have been either a pagan worshipping spot or a meeting place among the Celts.
Return along the B5320 for 400m (440yds).

6 King Arthur's Round Table

Despite its name there is no connection between this earthwork and ditch and the King Arthur of so many romantic legends. Again, it was probably some sort of meeting place among the Celts that originally resided in Cumbria.
Take the A6 south towards Clifton.

7 Clifton Hall Pele

At one time other buildings would have been attached to this 16th-century pele tower (*see pp102–3*), but today it is a solitary building preserved by English Heritage in testament to the days when the border wars were such that defensive towers were necessary to protect the local citizens.

A fallen sculpture in the ruins of Brougham Hall

LOWTHER

This village takes its name from the aristocratic family that have been resident here since the 13th century and it is dominated by their ancestral home, Lowther Castle.

Lakeland Bird of Prey Centre

Located within the castle grounds is this highly popular visitor centre focussing on all manner of birds of prey, from owls to eagles. The skills and techniques of falconry can be seen at their impressive best in the daily flying demonstrations held here. A joy for anyone with an interest in these magnificent birds.

Lowther Parklands. Tel: 01931 712746. Open: Apr–Oct daily 10am–5pm. Admission charge.

Lowther Castle

Although there has been a residence for the Lowther family (the Earls of Lonsdale) here for centuries, the current castle only dates from the early 1800s and was designed by Robert Smirke, the architect who would go on to create one of Britain's greatest buildings, the British Museum in London. All the towers and turrets were typical of the Neo-Gothic style of the day and lend an imperious air to the whole estate. But such extravagances are hard to maintain in the modern day and the family moved out of the castle in the 1950s. There is little that remains of the original interior other than the basic structure. The castle grounds, however, are now a public park.

Parklands: Tel: 01931 712523. www.lowther.co.uk. Open: Easter–May Sat–Sun 9am–5pm; June–mid-Sept daily 9am–5pm. Free admission.

ULLSWATER

The meandering 12km (7.5-mile) long lake that is Ullswater is one of the most popular in the region, with steamboats taking visitors on tranquil journeys along its route. The area rising up from the lake is one of the most impressive due to its mountains, popular with hikers in summer and even skiers in winter. Even Wordsworth was moved by this beautiful spot – his much-quoted poem 'Daffodils' was inspired by the spring flowers that lined the lakeside at Ullswater. Visit Glencoyne Bay in March or April to witness the same vision that gave rise to one of literature's most famous works.

ULLSWATER STEAMERS

The most popular attraction at Ullswater are the two 19th-century steam boats (now, however, operating on diesel), as well as a newer boat added in 2007, that ply the waters on a variety of cruises daily. The journey from Pooley Bridge in the north to Glenridding in the south (or vice versa) takes an average of two hours, offering peaceful reflective time to take in the beauty of the landscape. There are shorter cruises on offer too, and many are designed to combine with a walk along the banks of the lake as well as taking to the water.

The Pier House, Glenridding. Tel: 017864 82669. www.ullswater-steamers.co.uk. Open: daily. Admission charge.

Ullswater is very popular and draws many visitors

Aira Force

The main attraction of this landscaped park is the 21m (69ft) waterfall that gives it its name, but, courtesy of the National Trust, it also remains a lovely garden setting that was originally created by private owners in the late 18th century. There are a variety of walking trails and bridges that allow visitors to take in the many trees and plants, all with the beautiful view of Ullswater lake as a backdrop.

Helvellyn

The third-highest mountain in England at 950m (3,117ft) is perennially popular with hikers and scramblers wishing to reach the peak, where there is a 24m (79ft) deep pool known as the red tarn. However, the mountain is notoriously dangerous, particularly the uphill route known as the Striding Edge, so should only be undertaken by experienced climbers and in good weather.

Drive: River Eden

This drive takes in some of the most beautiful parts of eastern Cumbria, all the while following the route of the 145km (90-mile) long River Eden. The drive, which should take a full day if stopping at all the points, ends at Armathwaite in east Cumbria, but the river can be followed to its final destination at the Solway Firth in west Cumbria.

Distance 51km (32 miles).

Start the drive at Outhgill, on the B6259 road on the border with north Yorkshire, and head north.

1 Mallerstang Valley

This wonderful wild area, surrounded by high fells and some impressive waterfalls, is also home to an area known as Giant's Graves, believed to be burial mounds dating from prehistoric times. Marking the border with the Pennines to the east, it offers some of the most untrammelled walking country in the county, but be aware that the weather can often be as rough as the landscape.

Continue north along the B6259.

2 Pendragon Castle

Legend has it that this ruined castle was built in the 12th century by the father of King Arthur, Uther Pendragon, as part of a defence against the invading Saxons. What is known for sure, however, is that it has had a chequered history. Rebuilt after a Scottish raid in the 14th century, then again after a fire in the 17th

century by the redoubtable Lady Anne Clifford (*see p80*), it was gradually abandoned and by the end of the 18th century left in the derelict state that is seen today. But just walking amid its ruined walls conjures up images of the

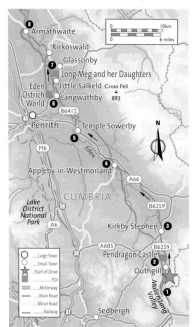

The River Eden at Appleby

many centuries of history that these stones have witnessed.
Continue north along the B6259.

3 Kirkby Stephen

This pretty market town (*see pp80–82*) makes an ideal stop for some refreshment before continuing with the drive, as there are plenty of cafés and tea rooms here.
Continue north along the B6259 then join the A66 northwards towards Appleby and Penrith.

4 Appleby-in-Westmorland

This pretty market town was one of the many places that Lady Anne Clifford (*see p80*) made her home, in Appleby

Castle, and she and her beloved mother are both buried in the town's church. Another historic former resident was 18th-century Prime Minister William Pitt the Younger, who took office at the age of 24 – the youngest prime minister in British history to this day. Today the town is also famous for its horse fair (*see p78*) and for being one of the stops on the popular Carlisle to Settle Railway (*see pp56–7*).
Continue north along the A66.

5 Temple Sowerby

This small village may now lie just off the unromantic A66 (and the creation of a bypass in 2007 was the result of

APPLEBY HORSE FAIR

In 1685 King James II established a charter allowing an annual horse fair to be held beside the River Eden, and this tradition has continued to this day in Appleby-in-Westmorland, making it one of the oldest surviving horse fairs in the country. Every June vast numbers of gypsies and travellers arrive just outside the town, ostensibly to trade horses but also as a social gathering among their communities. Travellers so often get a hostile reception from other members of society, but this is a festive event that celebrates their traditions, music and belief systems – this is the place to come if you want your fortune told in the time-honoured manner. One of the main traditions of the fair is the bareback horse and rider swimming event in the River Eden, but sadly in 2007 this ended in tragedy when one horse panicked and drowned. Controversy has also shadowed the event in recent years, as animal rights campaigners have complained that many of the horses are mistreated or malnourished by unscrupulous dealers, but both the police and RSPCA officials are always in plentiful attendance to help safeguard the horses' welfare.

much local campaigning), but it was once situated on the Roman road from York and a milestone from that period still stands. It was also once home to a group of Knights Templar, the medieval Christian crusaders, from whom it takes its name.
Continue for 1.5km (1 mile) along the A66 then turn right on to the B6412.

6 Langwathby

This charming village is big on tradition, with springtime maypole dancing and summertime scarecrow competitions.

It's also more popular with visitors than its size might suggest, being home to the Eden Ostrich World (*see p150*).
From Langwathby follow the signs for Little Salkeld.

7 Long Meg and her Daughters

The true origins of this impressive stone circle are unknown, but archaeologists have averaged its date to 1500 BC, during the Bronze Age. There are apparently 69 stones, of which Long Meg is the tallest at 3.5m (11^1/$_2$ft), but no one seems able to tot up their number completely – part of the folklore of the site is that if anyone can come up with a definitive number, bad luck will ensue (although the true reason is that some of the stones are now underground). The circle is thought to have got its current name after a local witch.
Follow the signs to Glassonby and Kirkoswald and continue north to Armathwaite.

8 Armathwaite

Just before you reach Armathwaite look out for the rather eerie faces carved into the cliffs south of the village. Armathwaite itself is a draw for anglers, because of its high salmon population. There is also a historic pele tower (*see pp102–3*) still standing in the village, right on the banks of the River Eden, although plenty of subsequent additions have been built up around it over the centuries.

A gypsy caravan arrives for the start of the Appleby Horse Fair

BROUGH

A small market town and former cotton-milling centre, Brough's economy also boomed in the 19th century when it was a popular stagecoaching stop with travellers journeying between England and Scotland.

Brough Castle

Yet another of Lady Anne Clifford's (*see below*) acquisitions, this early 12th-century castle had been in a state of disrepair since 1254 until Lady Anne's ancestor, Robert Clifford, arrived 14 years later and added a hall and tower to the structure. However, it again became neglected during the 16th century, until the arrival of Anne in the 17th century. It was built on the site of a former Roman fort and is notable for being built from stone – an innovation in Norman times. Today, however, it is once again in ruins – Clifford's family used much of the stone here to build new constructions in Appleby after her death – although what remains is protected by English Heritage. Also visible from the castle is the Fox Tower, a 17th-century folly, built by a wealthy local mill owner. Access to the site is free.

KIRKBY STEPHEN

The Monday market at Kirkby Stephen carries on a tradition that has been in place here since 1361 and in summer, particularly, it is popular with visitors. Evidence of Viking settlement in the area can be found in the parish church, where a 'loki stone' depicting a figure with horns (typical of the Norse period) can be found.

Little Salkeld Watermill

Locals have been milling grain in this area since the 12th century but this watermill dates from the mid-18th century. Its distinction is that it is still operational, milling grain into flour by traditional waterwheel methods rather than by machinery, and without the use of chemicals or additives. Tours of the mill allow visitors to see the sluice gate, the working wheels, the milling stones, and final product, fully explaining the

---

LADY ANNE CLIFFORD

Lady Anne Clifford (1590–1676), daughter of the Earl of Cumberland, was originally Yorkshire-born, being raised at Skipton Castle. Outraged that her inheritance passed to her uncle instead of herself on her father's death, she fought vehemently for the return of what she considered her money, finally succeeding in her claim in 1643. Despite her considerable old age for the time, she then devoted her life to acquiring and renovating what she considered to be worthwhile properties (castles) in the Cumbrian region, among them Brough, Appleby, Pendragon and Brougham (where she died), as well as a number of churches in the area. In honour of her vast contributions to the area and the historical buildings that she saved there is now a 160km (100-mile) walk named Lady Anne's Way, from Skipton to Brougham, which is signposted along the route and takes participants past the many towns and properties that she tirelessly salvaged from ruin. Sadly, however, following her death many of these places once again were decimated by either human hands or nature.

manner in which the flour is made. On site there is also a tearoom serving freshly baked breads made from the mill's own flour.

Little Salkeld. Tel: 01768 881523. www.organicmill.co.uk. Open: daily 10.30am–5pm, tours Mar–Oct Mon–Fri & Sun 2pm & 3.30pm. Admission charge for tours.

Nine Standards

Also featuring on Wainwright's Coast to Coast walk, this hill 5km (3 miles) outside Kirkby Stephen is named after the nine 3m (10ft) high cairns (stone columns) perched on the summit. As with so many ancient monuments, the purpose of the cairns and their position is unclear, but could be associated with the Romans (perhaps as a defensive measure), or even earlier with the Celts. Access to the stones is unhindered but care must be taken not to cause any

further damage to the delicate state of the stones.

Stainmore Railway

In the 1860s a railway line between Yorkshire and Cumbria was constructed primarily to carry goods from the mines in both regions. Higher speed lines, the demise of the mining industry and the construction of roads made it more and more obsolete in the second half of the 20th century, however, and the line closed in 1962. Today, however, there is a designated 5km (3-mile) walk, known as the Northern Viaducts Round, which is a must for any railway buffs and boasts lovely views of this stretch of the Eden Valley. The impressive Podgill and Merrygill viaducts have been restored and are a fine example of the engineering skills of the Victorian railway workers.

The keep at Brough Castle

Walk: The Poetry Path

Just outside Kirkby Stephen, along the banks of the River Eden, a so-called Poetry Path has been erected, featuring 12 poems by local poet Meg Peacocke carved into stone bollards. These carvings reflect a year in the life of a Cumbrian farmer and the long-standing agricultural traditions as well as more modern techniques.

The full walk is just under a mile and can be undertaken in about an hour.

From Kirkby Stephen walk along Nateby Road to Bollam Lane, where the first stone poem is on the right.

1 January

This is the time of year traditionally given over to hedge laying, a skill that has been practised for centuries as a means of enclosing livestock with a farm's boundaries.

Walk through the gate and cross the footbridge to the stone barn.

2 February

As the poem suggests, the long winter months are now beginning to take their toll on both farmers and their livestock, who have been kept inside in barns throughout the cold weather.

Continue along the track through the next gate and turn right to the stream for the next poem.

3 March

The poem here celebrates the flow of the stream, but the stone also details the ancient craft of dry stone walling. Winter weather can sometimes damage the stone so in March any gaps or repairs are undertaken.

Continue along the same track to the April stone.

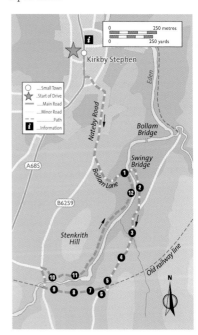

4 April

Sheep are the mainstay of Cumbria's agriculture and one of the most charming times to visit the region is the lambing season in April, when the babies gambol about after their mothers.
Walk to the stone bridge.

5 May

Shepherding is hard work, as this poem indicates. The elder sheep need to be checked for health reasons, the lambs need to be tagged and the sheepdogs are hard at work tending the flock.
Cross the bridge and follow the track to the right.

6 June

This is the month when the sheep are shorn, as the summer sun warms their newly clipped backs as they graze on their pastures.
Go through the gate on the right and follow the old railway line on the left.

7 July

As summer reaches its height tractors can be seen up and down the fields in the process of haymaking, used as fodder for livestock.
Continue on the track to the August poem on the right.

8 August

August is the traditional month for agricultural shows in Cumbria where the best sheep are awarded prizes, the faithful sheepdogs take part in trials, and local produce is sold at stalls.
Continue to the end of the railway line.

9 September

More socialising as well as serious business is done at the Farmers' Markets, where the spring lambs are either sold to other farmers or the already slaughtered meat is on sale.
At the bridge turn right and cross the River Eden continuing along the path, then take a right down to the river.

10 October

The poem reflects the mix of limestone and sandstone that makes up the geology of the area. This is also the month when markets are held to sell sheep ready for breeding and lambing the following spring.
Continue to the gate and turn left.

11 November

The sheep's breeding, known as tupping, begins. The farmer has to 'dip' the male tups with coloured grease so that he can see which ewes have possibly been impregnated by the residue of the grease on their wool.
This is the longest part of the walk – go through the gate and continue along the path over the two fields back to the gate that began the walk.

12 December

In the depths of winter, this is the time for farm maintenance, repairing any buildings or enclosures and possibly undertaking a bit of tree planting.

NENTHEAD

The lifeblood of Nenthead for more than 200 years was its lead and silver mining industry. This was managed from the early 18th century by the London Lead Company, who comprised Quakers. Therefore the village also benefited from the prescience and generosity of their managers, who took their social welfare very much into account – certainly not a common practice in the 18th and 19th centuries. This novel concept grew into a purpose-built village centred around the mines, with small but well thought-out cottages as miners' homes, a school for the miners' children, a shop, public baths and a chapel. There was even a free library – the first of its kind in England. The mines finally closed in the 1960s, like so many in the area. Today this small village's two main claims to fame are that it is one of the highest in England, perched at 457m (1,500ft) above sea level, and it is also on the C2C route, the 225km (140-mile) long-distance cycle route between the east and west coasts of northern England. Another spot on the C2C is the Hartside Pass, which offers one of the best views in England, taking in the mountains of Helvellyn (*see p75*) and Skiddaw, among others, all the way across to the border with Scotland.

Nenthead Mines Heritage Centre

Everything you wanted to known about the mining industry in the area as well as the history of living and working in Nenthead can be found at this excellent heritage centre. In former mining structures renovated for the purpose, there are a wide range of exhibits – many of them interactive – that uncover the geology of the region, the various mining techniques over the centuries and the boom then bust of the industry, as well as an exploration into many of the hardships and dangers of mining life. Part of the underground mine has also now been restored to enable underground tours along the various tracks and tunnels, which brings the imagination to life about what conditions must have once been like down there. There's also a panning area where you can try your hand at panning for minerals. Some of the miners' cottages have also now been turned into holiday accommodation. *Nenthead. Tel: 01434 382726. www.npht.com. Open: mid-Mar–Oct daily 11am–5pm. Admission charge.*

South Tynedale Railway

In order to be able to transport the lead that was being mined at Nenthead it was necessary to build a railway in the mid-19th century, which was operational for over 100 years. It closed in 1976 but in the early 1980s a narrow gauge line was constructed along a 3km (1¾-mile) part of its original route, from Alston to Kirkhaugh (although there are plans to extend this further to Slaggyford). Taking one of the restored steam trains on this short stretch is a magical journey of nostalgia. Also at

A monument to the miners at Nenthead

Alston Station is a model railway exhibit, and a shop that caters to all manner of railway enthusiasts.
Alston Railway Station. Tel: 01434 382828 (for timetable).
www.strps.org.uk. Open: Good Friday–July & Sept–Oct days vary; Aug daily. Admission charge.

SHAP

Limestone and granite quarrying are the main activities of the village of Shap, but there have been settlements around here since prehistoric times, as evidenced by the number of mysterious stone circles nearby. Most travellers journeying between England and Scotland will pass through the village, cut in two as it is by the A6 and M6, as well as the west coast railway line.

Keld Chapel

This unassuming-looking building is in fact a 15th-century chantry chapel, associated with the monastic order at Shap Abbey. At one time a private house, it is now preserved by the National

The West Tower of Shap Abbey

Trust. It was probably used as a place of worship for local villagers once the abbey at Shap had been dissolved during the reign of Henry VIII.

Keld. No phone. Open: daily – details of where to pick up the key are displayed on the chapel door.

Shap Abbey

Just outside the village is this lovely, although now somewhat ruined, 12th-century abbey, which was occupied by a brotherhood known as the Premonstratensian Canons, until Henry VIII's dissolution of the monasteries in the 16th century (this was the last of England's monasteries to go). The most distinctive aspect of the abbey is the West Tower, dating from the 15th century, which is also the most complete remnant of the site. There are also remains of the monks' cells and the Chapter House, but until the Victorians instilled the idea of preserving old buildings, little care or interest was taken over architectural history and much of the estate was destroyed by the taking of stones to build new edifices in the surrounding area.

Shap. No telephone. Open: daily. Free admission.

Sleddale Hall

One of the best-known films to have been partially shot in Cumbria is the 1987 cult classic *Withnail and I* (*see p19*), and the rather grand-sounding Sleddale Hall is the dilapidated cottage known as Crow Cragg, in which the two main characters, played by Richard E. Grant and Paul McGann, find themselves enduring a disastrous holiday with the lascivious Uncle Monty. Nearby is the stone bridge from which Withnail attempts to catch fish by shooting them with a gun. Its isolated position on the Wet Sleddale Reservoir can be visited from the outside, but it is privately owned so there is no public access inside.

TEBAY

Tebay became a popular stagecoach stop in the 18th century, and with the coming of the railway in the following century, it has a long history of being a travellers' resting place. It was also home to a lady named Mary Baynes, who became known locally as the Witch of Tebay, because she had premonitions of fast 'horseless' carriages – and indeed the London to Glasgow west coast route does now rattle past the village at some speed. In the 1970s came the M6 motorway and today it remains a popular stopping off point among motorists, largely because of the Tebay Services at Junction 38. This is the only family-run services in England and their commitment to employing only local people and local materials has never wavered. There's a hotel here that is quite a notch above any other motorway accommodation, but many people just stop to visit the farm shops on site, which sell the very best of local produce.

Tebay Services: Junction 38, M6. Tel: 015396 24944. Open: daily.

South Cumbria

Stately homes, historic abbeys and priories, even a Hollywood star all make up the attractions of South Cumbria, bordered by Lancashire and the sands of Morecambe Bay to the south and the edge of the Lake District National Park to the north.

Kendal is the main town in the area, with plenty to explore, but don't miss the opportunity to wander around the evocative ruins of castles and monasteries in their countryside setting, while gardening fans have a wealth of landscaped areas to visit during the summer months. Nostalgia is the order of the day in museums dedicated to local life, classic cars and industrial life. This is also the centre for the production of the famous Cumbrian crystal, which makes an ideal souvenir to take home from your visit.

KENDAL

Occupied since Roman times, and perhaps before, Kendal is one of the main towns in the Lake District and not only makes an ideal base for exploring the region but also has plenty of interest in its own right. There's a ruined Norman castle to explore, plenty of impressive Victorian architecture to admire, old mill workers' cottages from the time when it was the centre of the wool industry, as well as excellent museums. And, of course, don't forget to try its most famous product, the sweet confection that is Kendal Mintcake (*see p136*).

Abbot Hall Art Gallery & Museum of Lakeland Life

Set in a converted 18th-century mansion, Abbot Hall is considered by many to be the best art gallery in northwest England. Its collection covers artworks from the 18th to the 20th century, with paintings by John Constable, John Ruskin, Allan Ramsey, prints by Picasso and Matisse and sculpture by Barbara Hepworth, to name just a few. In addition, there's always a busy programme of touring exhibitions.

Across the grounds, in what were originally the stables for the house, there's an award-winning museum dedicated to life in the Lake District through the centuries. Recreated village

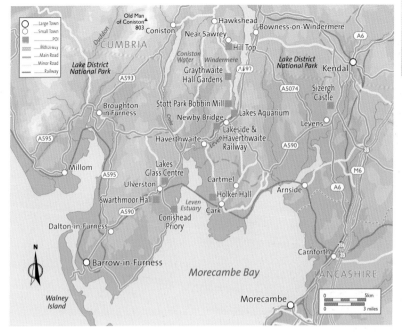

streets and home interiors from times gone by are fun to explore, there's a vast collection of costumes from the area, and specialist exhibitions dedicated to subjects such as Arthur Ransome (*see p41*) and Beatrix Potter (*see pp22–3*). There is a café and play area.
Abbot Hall, Kirland. Tel: 01539 722494. www.abbothall.org.uk. Open: Easter–end Oct Mon–Sat 10.30am–5pm; Nov–mid-Dec & mid-Jan–Easter 10.30am–4pm. Admission charge.
Museum: Tel: 01539 722464. www.lakelandmuseum.org.uk. Open: mid-Mar–Oct Mon–Sat 10.30am–5pm; Nov–mid-Dec & mid-Jan–mid-Mar Mon–Sat 10.30am–4pm. Closed: mid-Dec–mid-Jan. Admission charge.

Kendal Museum

Still going strong since opening in 1796, this small museum focuses on natural history, from a detailed explanation of the geography and geology of the Lake District itself, to an exploration of wildlife from all four corners of the globe, including a strong emphasis on conservation. The Wainwright Gallery, on the other hand (named after Alfred Wainwright, who was once a curator here), follows the human side of history, taking on the daunting task of exploring human life on Earth from prehistoric times to the 21st century.
Station Road. Tel: 01539 721374. www.kendalmuseum.org.uk. Open: Thur–Sat 12–5pm (last admission 4.30pm). Admission charge.

The Quaker Tapestry is on display in the Friends' Meeting House in Kendal

The Quaker Tapestry

Begun in 1982, this extraordinary 48m (157ft) long tapestry, embroidered by Quakers all over the world, details the history of the Religious Society of Friends, including some of its more prominent members over their 350-year existence. Even those with little or no interest in the society itself will marvel at the sheer scope and talent of the work, particularly those with knowledge of tapestry techniques. There's also a display of traditional Quaker costumes.

Friends Meeting House, Stramongate. Tel: 01539 722975. www.quaker-tapestry.co.uk. Open: Apr–Dec Mon–Fri 10am–5pm. Admission charge.

NEWBY BRIDGE

Newby Bridge, named after a 17th-century stone bridge over the River Leven, is most often visited because of its location at the south of Windermere (*see pp40–42*) or by those passengers taking the Lakeside and Haverthwaite Railway (*see p93*) but it has its own attractions nearby. One of the landmark buildings in the town is the Newby Bridge Hotel. Once a family home, it now proudly displays in the foyer letters written by William Wordsworth to the former residents, with whom he was friends.

Graythwaite Hall Gardens

Any budding gardener or horticulturalist will love a visit to these

GEORGE FOX AND THE QUAKERS

George Fox (1624–91) was an English dissenter who rejected the conventions and formalities of the Christian church and established Quakerism, a religious movement also known as the Society of Friends. Fox travelled both throughout the United Kingdom and abroad but it was at Pardshaw Crag in 1650 and in Ulverston, where he preached in 1652, that the ideas of Quakerism really began to take shape. Quakers did not have established buildings in which to gather and worship so they began to congregate at houses of fellow 'friends' and to this day Quaker buildings are referred to as 'meeting houses' rather than churches. The Swarthmoor Meeting House in Ulverston and Brigflatts, Sedburgh are still in use today, while in the Kendal Meeting House there is a large tapestry detailing the full history of the movement. As well as having devout beliefs, the Quakers were innovators in matters concerning the community, including social welfare, education and conservation.

19th-century gardens, landscaped with paths, statuary and herbaceous borders. Most impressive are the rhododendron bushes as well as the rose garden. The house itself is not open to the public. *Graythwaite. Tel: 01539 531333. www.graythwaite.co.uk. Open: Apr–Aug daily 10am–6pm. Admission charge.*

Lakes Aquarium

Celebrating not just the local lakes geography of Cumbria, but lakes all over the world, this has become one of the most popular indoor attractions in the area. There's an underwater tunnel that allows visitors to see perch, ducks and more from the waters of neighbouring Windermere, and still in local territory there are tanks with pike from the Leven Estuary and cod and even sharks from Morecambe Bay.

The famous gardens at Graythwaite Hall in Newby Bridge

Getting a close-up view in the underwater tunnel at the Lakes Aquarium

Moving on to warmer climes, however, there are the delightful otters of the Asian paddy fields, tortoises and catfish of Africa, piranhas of America and toads of the tropical rainforest regions. A great rainy day attraction to discover underwater goings on from around the world.

Lakeside. Tel: 01539 530153. www.lakesaquarium.co.uk. Open: daily 9am–6pm. Admission charge.

Lakeside & Haverthwaite Railway

This 6km (3.5-mile) stretch of the former Furness Railway that once ran all the way to Ulverston has been preserved as a heritage railway and runs regular services by steam train between Lakeside and Haverthwaite, and vice versa, via Newby Bridge. It's a short but highly pleasurable journey, taking in the lakeland scenery to the old-fashioned chuff of the steam engine. It's particularly fun for children, and there are quite often special events that are specifically geared towards kids. Visit the website for up-to-date timetables, many of which are arranged to fit in with the cruises on Lake Windermere.

Haverthwaite Station. Tel: 01539 531594. www.lakesiderailway.co.uk. Open: mid-Mar–Oct daily. Admission charge.

Stott Park Bobbin Mill

Weaving was one of the most important industries during the 19th century, largely based in neighbouring Lancashire, and Stott Park was established to produce the bobbins that held the wool and cotton on the weaving machinery. At its height the factory produced as many as 250,000 bobbins each week. Guided tours explain the working of the machinery and the manufacturing process, using much of the original equipment.

Off A590. Tel: 01539 531087. Open: Apr–Oct Mon–Fri 10am–5pm. Admission charge.

CARTMEL

This charming village of whitewashed houses, a 13th-century gatehouse (now a visitors' centre) and a market square, was traditionally a fishing village, sitting as it does almost on the northern shore of Morecambe Bay. But with the establishment of the priory in the 12th century it then became an important religious centre and this is still the main reason that visitors come here.

Cartmel Priory

Cartmel Priory was established in the 12th century by an order of Augustinian monks and thrived here for more than three centuries until Henry VIII's dissolution of the monasteries. The parish church, however, was saved, officially known as the Priory Church of St Mary and St Michael, and has been embellished and renovated many times so that a variety of architectural styles can be seen. The south doorway, chancel and transepts date from the original Norman period and there are a number of medieval tombs and statues, as well as sections of stained glass that were rescued from the damage caused during the dissolution. None of the monks' living quarters survived, but two doorways still exist that indicate the route between their cells and the church. Other notable features include carved columns and arches and a beautiful 17th-century choir stall.

Cartmel Park. Tel: 015395 36261. Open: daily. Tours Apr–Oct Wed 11am & 2pm. Free admission.

Holker Hall

Still home to the Cavendish family as it has been since the 17th century, this is a magnificent stately home that has opened some of its finest rooms to the public: the drawing room with its wonderful bay window and silk wallpaper, the billiards room with its oak table, oak again in the impressive staircase, the long gallery with, among other things, an antique rocking horse. Queen Mary's Bedroom is so named because she stayed at the house in 1937. Artworks in the house include paintings by Sir Joshua Reynolds and Van Dyck. As equally impressive as the house are its grounds, parts of which have been landscaped, with a vast array of plant species including a lovely rhododendron area. The highlight of the garden is the Great Holker Lime, one of the largest of its kind in the country. Every summer Holker Hall stages a popular festival in its grounds, featuring live music, arts and crafts and local food produce.

There has been a house here at Holker Hall since the early 16th century

*Cark-in-Cartmel. Tel: 015395 58328.
www.holker.co.uk. House. Open: mid-
Mar–Oct Sun–Fri 11am–4pm.
Gardens. Open: mid-Mar–Oct Sun–Fri
10.30am–5.30pm. Admission charge.*

Lakeland Motor Museum

Motoring buffs will be in their element
at this museum, in the grounds of
Holker Hall, devoted to the history of
the car, with classic models of Jaguars,
Fords, Cadillacs and more. There's also
a lovely re-creation of a garage as it
would have been in the pre-war years
with original signs, petrol pumps and
other equipment. Another highlight of
the museum is an exhibition dedicated
to Donald Campbell (*see pp38–9*) and
his father Malcolm, with replicas of the
Bluebird K7 in which Donald was killed
attempting to break the water speed
record. A video screening explains their
lives for those unfamiliar with these
remarkable men.
*Holker Hall, Cark-in-Cartmel.
Tel: 015395 58509.
www.lakelandmotormuseum.co.uk.
Open: Mar–Dec daily 10.30am–4.45pm;
Jan–Feb daily 10.30am–4pm.
Admission charge.*

ULVERSTON

Ulverston's glory years were during the
Industrial Revolution, when the world's
shortest canal was constructed in order
to transport goods the 1.5km (1-mile)
distance to the sea to the west for
export all over the world. It is still
home to many fine 18th- and 19th-
century buildings that are a reminder of
its economic heyday.

Conishead Priory

There has been a religious centre on this
site since the 12th century and the most
dominant building here is the 19th-
century Neo-Gothic house, but today the
main focus is on the Buddhist World
Peace temple and the Manjushri
Meditation Centre. The design of the
temple follows traditional Buddhist
principles of seeking the path to
enlightenment – four doors symbolise
the four gateways to spiritual
achievement and there is a dharma wheel
and a vajra on the roof, symbolising the
true Nirvana. Inside, too, there are more
symbols and inscriptions detailing the
Buddha's teachings, as well as a statue of
the man himself and his disciples.
*On the A5087. Tel: 01229 584029.
www.nkt-kmc-manjushri.org.
Open: Mon–Fri 9.30am–1pm, 2–5pm,
Sat 10am–noon. Free admission.*

Lakes Glass Centre

This isn't just a shopping experience.
Cumbrian crystal is admired the world
over and this is a chance to see some
the last craftsmen at work, blowing
glass into a wondrous array of shapes
and designs. There is, of course, a shop
on site if you want a gift or souvenir of
your visit to one of the country's last
lead crystal glassware factories.
*Cumbria Crystal. Tel: 01229 584400.
www.cumbriacrystal.com. Open:
Mon–Fri 9am–4.30pm. Free admission.*

Laurel and Hardy Museum

It may seem incongruous but the only museum in the world dedicated to one of Hollywood's best known and best loved comedy acts is located in Ulverston, the birthplace of one of its team, Stan Laurel. The museum not only covers the careers and films of the indomitable duo (including film screenings) but is full of their personal artefacts, from photographs and letters to larger belongings. Under the direction of legendary slapstick director Hal Roach, Cumbrian-born Stan Laurel (*see below*) and American Norvell ('Oliver') Hardy joined forces in the 1920s and went on to become one of the greatest comedy acts of all time. Anyone with an interest in old-time Hollywood won't help but raise a smile at the mad-cap antics on screen and the enduring friendship of two unlikely partners off screen.
Oubus Hill, next to Booth's.
Tel: 01229 582292.
www.laurel-and-hardy.co.uk.
Open: Feb–Dec daily 10am–4.30pm. Admission charge.

Swarthmoor Hall

For Quakers, this is considered the birthplace of the 'Society of Friends', as it was here that George Fox (*see p91*) composed his doctrine that still forms the basis of this 'religious' movement and it was here that the first 'meeting' was held (Quakers to this day do not worship in churches but in what are known as meeting houses). In fact, Fox married the lady of the house, Margaret Fell, after the death of her husband, who originally owned the house. Today Quakers still regard Swarthmoor as the root of their faith and it remains a popular visiting centre among the community.
Swarthmoor Hall Lane.
Tel: 01229 583204.
www.swarthmoorhall.co.uk.
Open: for tours: mid-Mar–mid-Oct Tue–Fri 2.30pm. Admission charge.

STAN LAUREL

They may be one of the most successful comedy double acts ever to have graced the silver screen, but one half of Laurel and Hardy had humble beginnings far from the bright lights of Hollywood. Stan Laurel (real name Arthur Stanley Jefferson) was born in the town of Ulverston in 1890 but caught the acting bug early as the son of a theatre manager. Joining a theatre company that took their work on tour to America, Laurel was intrigued by the burgeoning film industry and was offered a contract in Hollywood, never to return to England permanently again. He first teamed up with fellow comedy actor Oliver Hardy in 1927 and they fast became audience favourites in films such as *The Music Box* (1933), with its famous piano removal scene, and *A Chump at Oxford* (1939), but their popularity went into decline with the growing sophistication of cinema in the 1940s. Firm friends as well as professional partners, Laurel was distraught by the death of Hardy in 1957 and never performed again, eventually dying himself in 1965. But the familiar signature tune, the bowler hats, the slapstick antics and Laurel's bemused scratch of his head have stood the test of time, still raising laughter with modern day fans.

Celebrating Laurel and Hardy in Ulverston

Drive: Dalton-in-Furness to Barrow-in-Furness

Dalton-in-Furness has been a market town and an important centre since medieval times. Barrow-in-Furness, on the other hand, saw its fortunes rise during the Industrial Revolution due to its production of iron and steel. Its many beautiful Victorian buildings are a reminder of this.

The drive covers a distance of 16km (10 miles) and you should allow a day if you're to stop at all the sites.

Start this drive in the centre of Dalton-in-Furness.

1 Dalton Castle

In the centre of the town is this impressive pele tower, dating from 1330, which, like most of the pele towers in the region, was an important defensive measure against the Scots.
Leave Dalton from the north and follow the signs for the A590, taking the road westwards.

2 South Lakes Wild Animal Park

Animals from all over the world are kept at this open-air zoo. Viewing platforms allow a more personal experience with the beasts but in perfect safety (*see p151*).
Continue east along the A590 to the next roundabout and take the left exit, following signs for Furness Abbey.

3 Furness Abbey

The ruins of this 12th-century sandstone abbey, just outside Barrow, give little impression today of how influential and important it was during its heyday in the 14th and 15th centuries. The Cistercian monks here became rich by buying up local land, until King Henry VIII's dissolution of the monasteries in the 16th century. Among the ruins today, which have charmed such visitors as William Wordsworth, who mentions the place in his greatest work *The Prelude*, the west tower, the cloisters and the chapter house can still be seen. To gain more of an understanding of this evocative place, the visitors' centre details the history of the abbey and there is an audio tour available as you walk around the ruins.
Tel: 01229 823420. Open: Apr–Sept daily 10am–5pm; Oct–Mar Thur–Sun 10am–4pm. Admission charge.
Follow signs into the centre of Barrow-in-Furness.

4 The Dock Museum

This wonderful museum explores the history of shipbuilding, Barrow's most important industry, from the 19th century onwards. Possibly even more fascinating is the gallery devoted to life in Barrow as it changed at an incredible rate, learning about how locals and incomers coped with these changes. There's also a gallery exploring life in Barrow during World War II and displays of pieces of local archaeology, artworks and geology.

North Road. Tel: 01229 876400. www.dockmuseum.org.uk. Open: Easter–Oct Tue–Fri 10am–5pm, Sat & Sun 11am–5pm; Nov–Easter Wed–Fri 10.30am–4pm, Sat & Sun 11am–4.30pm. Admission charge. Leave Barrow on the A5087 and follow signs to Roa Island.

5 Piel Castle

This ruined island castle was built in the 14th century by the monks of Furness Abbey as a defensive measure to protect their land holdings on the Isle of Man, and their own monastery from invasion by Scottish raiders. One strange event in the castle's history is the arrival of a man called Lambert Simnel in 1487. He claimed to be heir to the English throne, and, although the rebellion was short lived, the island's only inhabitant – the landlord of the Ship Inn – is still known as the King of Piel. It is possible to visit the island and walk around the ruins, by taking a ferry from Roa Island (summer only).

Tel: 01229 475770. Open: daily. Free admission.

Drive: Dalton-in-Furness to Barrow-in-Furness

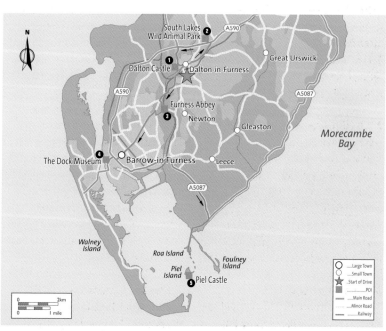

LEVENS

This unassuming village attracts visitors today because of its two historic houses.

Levens Hall and Gardens

This beautiful Elizabethan mansion was built at the end of the 16th century around a pele tower (*see pp102–3*) that had existed here since the Middle Ages. It is still a private residence, home to the Bagot family since the 19th century, who continue to lovingly preserve its heritage and have opened some of the more spectacular rooms to the public. These include a stunning oak-panelled drawing room and bedrooms with original four-poster beds and wallpaper. At the end of the 17th century the then resident Colonel James Grahame employed a French gardener (who had trained at Versailles) at Levens Hall and together they created the enchanting gardens that can still be seen today. Particularly impressive are the many topiary hedges, but there is also a lovely rose garden, a herb garden and a fountain area. Beyond the gardens is a large park, lined with oak trees and home to resident deer and goats. There's also a collection of early 20th-century steam engines in the grounds.

Levens. Tel: 01539 560321.
www.levenshall.co.uk.
House. Open: Apr–Sept Sun–Thur 12–4.30pm.
Gardens. Apr–Sept Sun–Thur 10am–5pm. Admission charge.

Sizergh Castle

This is another Tudor private home that was also built up around a medieval pele tower. It is still lived in by the original Strickland family, although much is now preserved by the National Trust. Inside are many pieces of original antique furniture and stained glass, but the highlight is the Inlaid Chamber, decorated with some of the most beautiful oak panelling in the country and a decorative plaster ceiling.

The 6ha (14 acres) of gardens, with their lakes and rock gardens, are also not to be missed. These are at their best in spring, when the new blooms arrive, and autumn, when the rust-coloured foliage lends a beautiful glow to the whole estate.

Sizergh. Tel: 01539 560951.
Castle. Open: mid-Mar–Oct Sun–Thur 1–5pm.
Garden. Open: mid-Mar–Oct Sun–Thur 11am–5pm. Admission charge.

The gardens at Levens Hall

Sizergh Castle incorporates a 14th-century pele tower

Pele Towers

During the 13th century Cumbria (or Cumberland and Westmorland, as the region was known then) found itself at the brutal heart of the ongoing battles between England and Scotland, mainly beginning with King Edward I (1272–1307) consistently attempting to seize power north of the border from the Scottish monarchy, notably against Robert the Bruce in the last year of Edward's life. Caught between these 'wars' the Lake District, as well as other border regions, witnessed slaughters and destruction as the two opposing sides fought out their ambitions. In later years they were also under threat from the border reivers (*see pp66–7*) as well as the two nations as a whole. Cumbrians fairly soon realised that they needed a plan to better protect themselves in these troubled times.

Often nicknamed 'poorman's castles' because they were constructed in previously unfortified towns by everyday people rather than royalty or the well-to-do, locals began to construct pele (sometimes called peel) towers – tall, square, thick-walled structures, smaller than but along the lines of a fortress, that were designed to be both defensive buildings as well as watch towers to look out for any advancing armies. Arrows and other weapons could be launched from the roof or warning fires lit, while the stories below (typically three) contained living quarters for the main chieftains of the region and shelter for livestock. They were also, if need be, a vital point of refuge for the local population if invaders attacked en masse. Another aspect vital to their design was the difficulty of access, usually through a small arch or simply a ladder, which further protected those hiding within, and windows were small and few in number. Occasionally they were surrounded by a moat, although more often than not such an elaborate addition was not within means.

In more rural areas, bastles were built rather than peles – smaller towers that were meant only as refuge points and were not permanent residences.

In ensuing centuries, when times were more peaceful after the Union of the Crowns between England and Scotland in the 17th century and defences were no longer required, many of the surviving towers were converted for other means. Some, such as Muncaster near Ravenglass and Levens Hall in Kendal (*see p100*), were extended into stately homes for aristocratic families, and many of these spectacular interiors and grounds are now open to the public. Others were converted into bell towers or extra buildings for churches, such as the Prior's Tower at Carlisle Cathedral (*see pp58–9*). Some, sadly, were left to ruin but are still an evocative and, in some ways, romantic reminder of this troubled past. As well as Cumbria, pele (adapted from pale, as in stake) towers survive in Northumberland (Northumbria), Lancashire and the Lothians in Scotland.

Levens Hall is one of the many large houses that have been built around older pele towers

West Cumbria

West Cumbria is defined by its coastline, bordering the Irish Sea. Long sandy beaches and the cold but calm waters have made this a popular seaside holiday area since visiting the seaside came into vogue in the 19th century. It is the place to head for if you are looking for a more tranquil break, whether that's taking in the bracing sea air or wallowing in the beautiful agricultural scenery of the inland valleys such as Eskdale or Ennerdale.

The coastal location also meant that the area, once defined by small local fishing communities, witnessed unprecedented prosperity and expansion, first by the ports that saw the arrival of cargo ships from the Americas, and then with the boom in the mining and steel industries. Although the area's once-thriving mines have now closed their pits (some are now heritage centres), the remnants of their success can still be seen in much of the architecture, from humble miners' cottages to grand Georgian and Victorian buildings commissioned by the aristocratic families who profited most from the trade.

RAVENGLASS

With its wide shingle beach and views out across the Irish Sea, Ravenglass is one of the main seaside towns of Cumbria. In Roman times it had some significance as a seafaring port, but the only boat activities you're likely to see here today are pleasure craft or the odd local fisherman.

Muncaster Castle and Gardens

A castle has stood on this site since 1258 and is still in the hands of the original family, the Penningtons. Alterations have been made to the original building, with the addition of a pele tower in the 13th century, and, in true Victorian style, considerable changes made to the design of the current drawing room. Features of the house include the Tapestry Room, named after the Flemish tapestry hanging here, and more notably its status as haunted – if you dare, there are opportunities to spend the night in this room. There is also a drinking bowl, thought to have belonged to King Henry VI, who took refuge here in 1464, in the castle. The castle's gardens are another highlight, divided in to various sections: a vegetable garden, an ornamental garden, even a secret garden. Muncaster is also home to a charity known as the World Owl Trust, and in the owl centre many different varieties of rescued owls can be seen, with flying displays in good weather.

On the A595. Tel: 01229 717614. www.muncaster.co.uk.

Castle. Open: mid-Feb–end Oct Sun–Fri 12–4.30pm; Dec Sun 5pm for Victorian Tour.

Gardens and Owl Centre. Open: mid-Feb–end Oct daily 10.30am–6pm; Nov–end Dec daily 11am–4pm. Closed: Jan–mid-Feb. Admission charge.

Ravenglass & Eskdale Railway

Like so many of the 19th-century railways that were originally built to carry industrial goods between areas, 11km (7 miles) of this rail track has been preserved as a scenic tourist activity. Renovated steam trains puff along the track that runs between Ravenglass, past Muncaster Hill, Irton Road, Eskdale, Fisherground and Beckfoot, to its destination, Dalegarth. Highlights of the route are views of Scafell Pike (*see pp51–3*) and other hills and fells, rolling farmland with sheep grazing in the fields, and bird watching at Barrow Marsh.

On the A595. Tel: 01229 717171. www.ravenglass-railway.co.uk. Open: year-round – phone or check website for timetables. Admission charge.

Roman Bath House

Anyone interested in England's Roman heritage should not miss the remarkable ruins of the Roman bath house. Thought to date from AD 130, the layout of the bath house within the

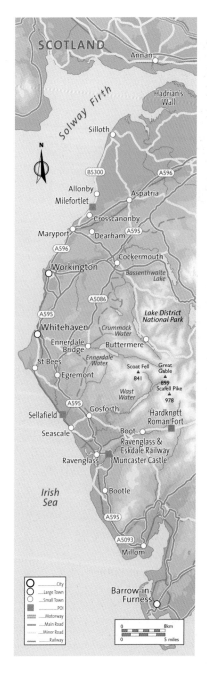

The Ravenglass and Eskdale Railway steam train

4m (13ft) high walls can still be made
out, including steam room areas.
Information panels help guide the
visitor through the site.
Ravenglass. Open: daily. Free admission.

MARYPORT

Like Ravenglass, Maryport was a Roman
port, but little became of this small
town whose main industry was fishing,
until the 18th century, when it became
an important centre for the coal
industry. Fishing is still relevant today,
however, and the harbour is always full
of small fishing craft and nets.

Lake District Coast Aquarium

Looking out as it does over the Irish
Sea, it's only fitting that Maryport's
harbour should be home to an
aquarium examining the sea life that
can be found in those waters. Mullet,
sea bass, dogfish, rays and turbot are
just some of the fish that can be seen
here in separate areas according to their
natural environment. There's even an
area that recreates the underwater
atmosphere of a shipwreck, which is
named in honour of local legend
Fletcher Christian. To keep children
amused who may tire of room after
room of fish, there's a pool in which
they can race radio-controlled boats,
and another shipwreck theme in the
outdoor adventure playground.
South Quay. Tel: 01900 817760.
www.lakedistrict-coastaquarium.co.uk.
Open: daily 10am–5pm.
Admission charge.

SELLAFIELD

One of the most controversial features on the
British landscape is the nuclear fuel
reprocessing site and power station known as
Sellafield. It was established under the name
of Windscale in the late 1940s, when nuclear
weapons began to be produced, and has been
in operation ever since. Unfortunately, more
than 20 accidents involving radioactive
matter escaping have occurred since 1950,
including the alarming Thorp Plant leak in
2005, with evidence of contamination in the
landscape and in wildlife. Investigations have
revealed that there is a higher than average
number of leukaemia cases for people living
in the vicinity of the plant. Nevertheless, as
long as Britain remains a nuclear power, sites
such as Sellafield may be a necessary evil,
and, in its favour, it can be argued that the
plant provides a large number of jobs for the
local community that would otherwise be
racked with unemployment.

Maritime Museum

Everything to do with Maryport's
maritime history can be found here,
from model boats, to telescopes, to a
whale's tooth, to exhibitions on
Fletcher Christian (*see p108*). There are
plenty of paintings with a maritime
theme, too. A small but involving
collection for anyone interested in
sailing and shipping.
1 Senhouse Street. Tel: 01900 813738.
Open: Mon–Sat 10am–4pm.
Free admission.

Senhouse Roman Museum

During the time of Emperor Hadrian
(*see p60*) the Romans built one of the
largest forts in northern England in
what is now Maryport. This museum

Maryport's harbour is busy with fishing boats

(named after the Senhouse family who created the modern town over the centuries), situated next to what was once the fort, contains archaeological finds discovered on the site, including an important collection of military altar stones. It also details the full extent of the site, which was not only home to soldiers but Roman civilians, too, and included, among other things, a bath house, temples and barracks. The museum also has an observation

FLETCHER CHRISTIAN

Fletcher Christian (1764–93), immortalised by the actor Marlon Brando in the 1962 film *Mutiny on the Bounty*, was born near Maryport in the village of Dearham and attended school in St Bees. He first took to the seas at the age of 18, but it was his 1788 voyage to Tahiti, aboard the HMS *Bounty* under the command of Captain William Bligh, that would turn him into the stuff of legend. Having collected their intended cargo of breadfruit and set sail to return to England, Christian and 18 co-mutineers overcame Bligh in his cabin and ordered him off the ship along with his followers. Quite why the mutiny took place is not clear but remarkably Bligh managed to navigate them in a small boat to Timor, and made his way home to England, where he reported the mutiny. Meanwhile the mutineers, aware that they might be sought by the navy, sailed the *Bounty* to Pitcairn Island where, initially, a harmonious community was established with Christian at the helm. But soon relationships soured between the locals and the incomers and in 1793 a battle commenced that supposedly saw many of the men shot, including Christian, although there have always been conspiracy theories that he escaped, either to another island or back to England. To this day there are inhabitants on Pitcairn Island with the surname Christian.

tower, which allows visitors to look out of the original position of the fort with a bird's-eye view.
The Battery, Sea Brows.
Tel: 01900 816168.
www.senhousemuseum.co.uk.
Open: Wed–Thur, Sat–Mon 10.30am–5.30pm, Fri 10.30am–8pm. Admission charge.

WHITEHAVEN

As with Maryport, Whitehaven escalated from a sleepy fishing community to an extremely important town due to the Industrial Revolution and advancing coal mining and shipbuilding industries. Towards the end of the 17th century much of the modern town that can be seen today began to be built up by the Lowther family of Lowther Castle (*see p74*), and houses, churches and piers began to be erected. It was also an important import area, bringing in tobacco, sugar and rum from the Americas to be transported to the rest of the country.

The Beacon

Pretty much anything you wanted to know about Whitehaven can be uncovered in the town's main museum, right on the harbour front. There's a full explanation of the history of the town and the lives of the people within it over the centuries, covering such topics as children's games, costumes, and public health, as well as an area

The harbour at Whitehaven

devoted to the hardships of life in the town during World War II. There's also a nature aspect to the town, exploring the native wildlife, sealife and geology that makes up the port. The gallery area on the first floor is a must for art lovers, with regular touring exhibitions. *West Strand. Tel: 01946 592302. www.thebeacon-whitehaven.co.uk. Open: Tue–Sun 10am–4.30pm (last entry 3.45pm). Admission charge.*

Haig Colliery Mining Museum

Although mining in this area began in the 13th century it wasn't until the late 17th century that it started to become a major industry that would bring wealth and advancements to the region and the country. Haig Colliery, which closed in 1986 along with so many of England's mines, was, in its heyday, one of the most important deep mines. Now turned into a museum, it's possible to explore all aspects of mining, from the equipment, such as the winding engines, to the shafts, to the lives of the workers. The callousness of the mine owners can be seen in the area that details the risks and disasters that often befell the men and boys who went underground, many being killed in explosions or other accidents in the days when both safety measures and social welfare were not what they are today. One of the most evocative ways to understand what life must have been like is to visit the Oral History section, where former employees recount their memories and experiences.

Solway Road, Kells. Tel: 01946 599949 www.haigpit.com. Open: daily 9am–4.30pm. Admission charge.

The Rum Story

Georgian and Victorian gentlemen may have revelled in this new-found tipple but the story of the arrival of rum on British shores, excellently conveyed in one of Cumbria's best museums, is an often heart-rending and dangerous tale. Starting in the African villages, where innocent men were taken as slaves to the Caribbean on ships with terrible conditions, it moves on to a recreated rainforest and a sugar cane workshop in Antigua, where the men suffered dreadfully under both the working conditions and the treatment of the plantation owners. Even back in England, despite the decadence of the Punch Houses that were springing up, the rum ships were at threat from smugglers and pirates, and in America in the early 20th century, gang crime emerged during the smuggling of the Prohibition era. It's all quite a tale for just a bottle of rum. There are also displays on how rum is actually made, from cane field to bottle, and the cooperage of the barrels in which the liquid was originally transported, as well as details of the Jefferson family who originally ran the company and shop in which the museum is now set.

Lowther Street. Tel: 01946 592933. www.rumstory.co.uk. Open: daily 10am–4.30pm. Admission charge.

A statue at Whitehaven harbour commemorating a raid led by John Paul Jones during the American War of Independence

Cumbria's Industrial Revolution

It's not exactly new to say that the Industrial Revolution that took place during the 18th and 19th centuries changed the face of the world in so many ways, but what is interesting is to home in on smaller areas where new industries changed whole communities.

Mining had been a feature in Cumbria since the 16th century, but it was the advancements in equipment and techniques two and three centuries later, as well as the arrival of the railways, that allowed coal, iron and more to be transported to other regions and abroad and saw the industry rise to be an economic boon. Like its neighbouring county Northumbria, Cumbria had several collieries in areas such as Whitehaven (see p109) and Nenthead (see p84), which generally thrived until the industry was decimated during the Thatcher years of the 1980s. The geological landscape of the region also allowed for plentiful iron, slate, zinc and lead mining, the latter giving rise to the birth of the pencil, which also brought much prosperity to the area in the 19th century. Most of the mines, however, closed their doors in the 1960s – the cost of running mining operations had escalated and it became cheaper to import than to export.

Leather and textiles were also important industries at this time. Tanneries were successful in Cumbria because there were plentiful cattle supplies, as well as an abundance of oak trees, whose bark produces the tannin traditionally used in the process of turning animal skin into leather. So much woodland also allowed for many other industries to flourish, including charcoal production and cooperage (barrel-making), but one of the most distinctive new occupations in the area was the production of bobbins. The cotton industry was one of the largest during the Industrial Revolution, and every cotton mill needed bobbins, and plenty of them. Cumbria's coppice wood was ideal for this, and during the 19th century there were more than 80 mills employing skilled workers dedicated solely to the production of bobbins. But again, times change – new machinery and the switch from wooden to mass-produced metal bobbins saw the industry fall almost as quickly as it arose. Although there were a few cotton mills in the area, the main cloth produced in Cumbria was linen,

The Dock Museum in Barrow-in-Furness commemorates the town's once-thriving shipbuilding industry

made from locally grown flax, as well as sackcloth, ropes and more made from locally grown hemp. Although there were large factories in this field, a lot of the work was done through cottage industries, with local women spinning yarn in their own homes ready for factories to merely concentrate on the actual weaving.

Wood, again, was vital to another industry, paper making, with successful mills located in towns such as Cockermouth and Maryport. A few specialist paper makers remain in Cumbria even today.

One of the most important advancements of the Industrial Revolution, however, was transport, without which many of these businesses could not survive in any more than a local context.

Shipbuilding was an important industry on the west coast, as well as submarine manufacturing in Barrow-in-Furness from the end of the 19th century. The arrival of the railways revolutionised not only industry, but also the movement of populations, which in turn brought tourism to the Lakes. Cumbria remains one of the best areas of Britain to see preserved Victorian steam railways, in places such as Ravenglass (see p105).

Drive: West coast beaches

Cumbria's coastline is often overlooked by visitors, yet it offers several historical sights, almost deserted beaches and a chance to escape the crowds that are an inevitable summer curse in areas such as Windermere and Coniston. If you would rather explore with the wind in your hair, the West Cumbria Cycle Network takes in many of the places in this drive.

Distance: 100km (62 miles). Allow a full day.

1 Silloth
With views across the Solway Firth to Scotland, and across the Irish Sea, there are few better places to begin a drive exploring England's northwest coast. Take in the views from the area known as The Green, with a backdrop of the impressive Christ Church.
Join the B5302 until it joins the B5300 and drive south for 11km (7 miles).

2 Allonby
A popular resort since the 18th century, as attested by the Bath House in the town, this long stretch of sand makes for a lovely stroll. Alternatively, take to the water on a windsurfing board, if the weather is right.
Continue south on the B5300 for 5km (3 miles).

3 Crosscanonby
Milefortlet, a former Roman fort, is now a World Heritage Site and some of the layout of the military stronghold can still be seen. The 17th-century saltpans, which produced salt for the rest of the country, are also preserved.
Continue south on the B5300 until it meets the A596 and follow signs for Maryport for 5km (3 miles).

4 Maryport
One of the coast's main towns with both a Roman past and strong maritime history, some say Maryport also has some of the best fish and chip shops in northwest England! (*See p107.*)
Continue south on the A596 to the roundabout and take the second exit on to the B5296, a total of 10km (6 miles).

5 Workington
For a long time known as a steel-making town, the most historic building here is Workington Hall, with its medieval pele tower that once offered refuge to Mary, Queen of Scots.
Return to the A596 then turn right on to the A595 and right again on to the A5094 to Whitehaven, total distance 12km (8 miles).

6 Whitehaven

The main town on the Cumbrian coast, with a long history of mining and port activities, the main focus is the harbour area, which has been much improved in the past decade (*see pp108–9*).
From Lowther Street (A5094) continue to Scotch Street and drive south on the B5345 for 7km (4 miles).

7 St Bees

Originating from a 9th-century priory, St Bees is now one of the most popular resorts along this coast. The cliffs of St Bees Head are a favourite with walkers.
Continue south on the B5345 for 7km (4 miles) to turn right on to the A595 for another 7km (4 miles), then right on the B5344 for 5km (3 miles).

8 Seascale

Despite its close proximity to the Sellafield Nuclear Station (*see p107*), with its sandy beaches, fishing piers and watersports opportunities, Seascale remains as popular as ever.
Return to the B5344 and after 5km (3 miles) rejoin the A595. After 21km (14 miles) join the A5093 for another 5km (3 miles).

9 Millom

The history of Millom's iron ore mining is explored in the small Millom Folk Museum, with items of equipment and recreations of miners' cottages.
Station Road. Tel: 01229 772555.
Open: Apr–Sept Mon–Fri 10.30am–5pm.
Admission charge.

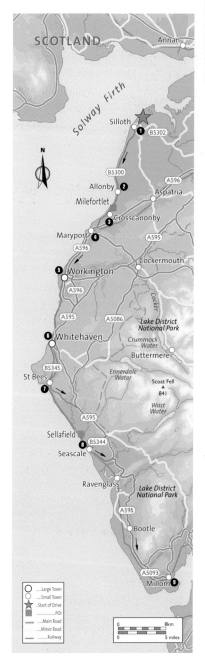

ESKDALE AND GOSFORTH

Eskdale Valley is best known for the Ravenglass and Eskdale Railway (*see p105*) but it's also a popular walking destination, through the rolling countryside with its many trails. Gosforth village has several historic buildings, as well as its famous cross.

Eskdale Mill

Remarkably this corn mill, on the outskirts of the village of Boot, was in commercial operation from 1578 until 1955. It is now preserved by a heritage trust because of its great historic significance, but the mill is not the only attraction – the views from its site are some of the best in the valley.

Boot. No tel. Open: daily. Free admission.

Gosforth Cross

The small village of Gosforth contains on of the most significant Viking monuments in England. In the cemetery of St Mary's Church, the carved 4.5m (14ft) high cross dates from AD 940 and combines Christian elements with pagan. The ash tree carved at the base of the cross is symbolic of how the Vikings believed the universe was run, but there are also details of Christ's Crucifixion, which indicates that the cross dates from the period when the Norse warriors were beginning to forsake mythology for Christian values. Inside the church itself are two further Viking stones that are thought to be ancient gravestones.

Eskdale is beautiful in almost any weather

A view over Ennerdale Water

Hardknott Roman Fort

Hardknott Roman Fort, on the Hardknott Pass, was situated on what was once a fairly important Roman road, and the fort was in part established to safeguard this route. The layout of many of the original buildings and areas, dating from AD 120 and once home to some 500 soldiers, including the bath house, a parade ground and the commandant's house, can still be made out. There are noticeboards at each site to help guide the visitor and explain each section. Note that although the site is open all year round, the road to the fort can be treacherous in winter or bad weather.

ENNERDALE AND EGREMONT

The peaceful village of Ennerdale Bridge and its surrounding valley are popular with both holidaymakers looking for tranquillity, and walkers, particularly in the area's forested woodlands. The small town of Egremont dates from the 13th century and is best known for its castle.

Egremont still upholds a charming medieval tradition every September during its Crab Fair. Despite its name this is nothing to do with crustaceans, but with crab apples, and is thought to date from the time when Lord Egremont supplied the locals with apples from his orchard at harvest time. Selected locals throw crab apples to spectators during the Parade of the Apple Cart through the town, followed by various agricultural events and the bizarre but hilarious World Gurning Championships (pulling faces).

The ruins of Egremont Castle

Egremont Castle

Egremont Castle was built in the 12th century on a hill above the town but fell in to ruin from the 16th century. It maintains a looming presence, however, and parts of the original building, such as the gatehouse, can still be seen. *Open: daily. Free admission.*

Ennerdale Water

Surrounded by forested land of pine and conifer trees, the lake at Ennerdale, stretching 4.5km (2¾ miles) in length is one of the most peaceful areas in the whole of Cumbria. There are plenty of marked walking trails around the lake and within Ennerdale Forest, but if you're not feeling energetic, it's simply a

SHEEP FARMING

Sheep farming is extremely important to Cumbria agriculturally and economically, with an estimated population of three million sheep at any one time. While numerous breeds successfully make their home on the fells, there are three that are particularly associated with the region: the Herdwick (so beloved by Beatrix Potter), the Rough Fess and the Swaledale. These hardy breeds are well suited to the hilly landscape and cold weather. Each flock has their own grazing land, known as a 'heaf', to which they remain fiercely loyal. Originally the sheep were valuable for both their meat and their wool, but wool prices have dropped to an almost worthless level and mutton, the meat of fully grown sheep, is not as much in favour in the British diet as it once was. Their main value today is in the lambs, born in the spring and sold at market for meat in the summer months.

beautiful place to bring a picnic and take in the panorama around you.

Lowes Court Gallery

Combining the tourist information centre with an art gallery exhibiting the work of local artists and craftworkers, today the Lowes Court Gallery is an eclectic mix of paintings, ceramics, carved wooden items, tapestries, handmade toys and much more, all here to celebrate Cumbrian artistry. *12 Main Street, Egremont. Tel. 01946 820693. www.lowescourtgallery.co.uk. Open: Mar–Dec Mon–Sat 10am–5pm (closes 1pm Wed); Jan–Feb Mon–Sat 10am–1pm. Free admission.*

Sheep need their thick coats here in winter

Getting away from it all

If on a longer visit to northern Britain you have a desire to see a bit more of the area, there are four obvious options – all within easy reach and each with its own distinctive character and beauty that deserve the attention of any visitor.

Isle of Man

A three-and-a-half hour ferry ride from Heysham in Lancashire, just south of Cumbria, across the Irish Sea (*www.steampacket.com*) brings visitors to the laid-back atmosphere of the Isle of Man, a crown dependency of the United Kingdom that operates its own government and legal system. The capital, Douglas, is obviously the most lively destination, with a charming harbour front and, in summer, horse-drawn trams recalling times gone by. Other highlights include the 13th-

Port Erin Bay in the southwest of the Isle of Man

Alnwick Castle is one of Northumbria's historic sites

century castle in Castletown, the 'living museum' of Cregneash that preserves many Manx traditions (Manx being the name of the island people) and the beaches of Port Erin and Port St Mary. The island is also famous for its Manx cats, a breed with no tail, many of which can be seen in the towns and villages as well as on plenty of postcards.

Northumbria

Having regularly suffered similar fates as Cumbria as a border region between the battles of Scotland and England, Northumbria, on Britain's east coast, is unsurprisingly full of history in its own right, and defensive castles, some now in ruins, abound. Traditionally, Northumbria was the great coal-mining district of Britain following the Industrial Revolution, but this was seriously decimated in the 1980s and a great deal of the area fell into an economic decline from which it is only just starting to emerge. Driving 92km (57 miles) east from Carlisle on the A69, along the route of the River Tyne, brings one to the region's economic heart, Newcastle upon Tyne. Named after an 11th-century castle, the city has had a chequered fortune in the past few decades but it has recently risen from the ashes as one of the country's most lively nightlife scenes, all under the floodlit gaze of its main symbol, the steel Tyne Bridge. Not far from the city, a full explanation of the life of a coal miner can be found at Britain's best open-air museum, **Beamish**. Recreating local life from the 18th century to the turn of the 20th century, mines, miners' cottages, shops and a school all present an authentic idea of the highs and lows of Northumbrian life in days gone by.

The cultural heart of the Northumbria region is **Durham**, best known for its Norman cathedral, as well as an 11th-century castle. It is also home to one of Britain's most reputed universities, so there's a student buzz around the medieval lanes and alleyways for much of the year.

Walkers are a frequent sight in Northumbria as they undertake the famous Pennine Way route, which travels from Derbyshire, past the Cheviot Hills here, and on to Scotland. Two castles of note are **Alnwick** and **Warkworth**, both homes of the Percy family, the dukedom of Northumbria (Northumberland) – Warkworth was used as the location setting for *Elizabeth*, the 1998 film starring Cate Blanchett as a young Queen Elizabeth I.

The Northumbrian coast has pleasant resorts such as Whitley Bay and Whitburn. Lindisfarne, the so-called Holy Island that was the site of a Celtic monastery is another major attraction, and is separated from the mainland each day at high tide. One of the most recent and controversial additions to the Northumbrian landscape is the 'Angel of the North', a vast 20m (66ft) high steel sculpture, with wings stretching to 54m (178ft), created by the sculptor Antony Gormley. Erected in 1998, standing on a hill beside the A1 near Gateshead, its reception has always been divided between admirers and detractors.

Beamish Open Air Museum: Beamish. Tel: (0191) 370 4000. www.beamish.org.uk. Open: mid-Mar–Oct daily 10am–5pm (last admission 3pm); Nov–mid-Mar Tue–Thur, Fri–Sun 10am–4pm (last admission 3pm). Admission charge. Durham Cathedral: The College, Durham. Tel: (0191) 386 4266. www.durhamcathedral.co.uk. Open: Mon–Sat 7.30am–6pm, Sun 7.45am–5.30pm. Free admission. Alnwick Castle: Alnwick. Tel: (01665) 510777. www.alnwickcastle.com. Open: Apr–Oct daily 11am–5pm. Admission charge. Warkworth Castle: Warkworth. Tel: (01665) 711423. www.warkworth.co.uk. Open: Apr–Sept daily 10am–5pm; Oct daily 10am–4pm; Nov–Mar Sat–Mon 10am–4pm. Admission charge.

Scotland

Having suffered for centuries by nature of its border position, just north of Cumbria, across the Solway Firth, is the now peaceable land that is Scotland. Since the devolution of its parliament in 1999, debates have raged as to whether it will once again become an independent country, but for now it remains a part of Great Britain, albeit with a highly individual spirit. Just over an hour's drive, 160km (100 miles) up the M74 motorway from Carlisle, or

St Mary's Loch in the Scottish Borders

two and a half hours by train (*www.firstgroup.com/scotrail*), brings one to Glasgow, Scotland's largest city. Once purely industrial and working-class, it is now rejuvenated and renowned for its wonderful museums and art galleries, as well as many architectural gems by the great Art Nouveau architect and designer Charles Rennie Mackintosh. A little further north is the area known as The Trossachs, whose mountains and valleys make wonderful walking country, while Loch Lomond, Britain's largest freshwater lake, is one of the country's most popular tourist destinations. To the east is Scotland's capital, Edinburgh, considered by many to be Britain's most beautiful city, with its fascinating juxtaposition between medieval history and Georgian elegance, and its striking cliff-top castle. Between the two is the historic town of Stirling, famous for William Wallace's victory against the English in 1297, depicted somewhat imaginatively in the film *Braveheart*, and also with a striking hilltop castle.

Scotland is, of course, most famous for its highland region of dramatic mountains looming down over romantic lochs, including Loch Ness, the debatable home to the world's most famous monster. Offshore, the Western Isles or Hebrides offer some of the remotest communities in Britain, where in many cases time seems to have stood still amid the hardy farmers and fishermen.

Edinburgh Castle: Castle Hill, Edinburgh. Tel: (0131) 225 9846. Open: Apr–Oct daily 9.30am–6pm; Nov–Mar daily 9.30am–5pm. Admission charge.

Glasgow has been transformed in the last twenty years

Yorkshire

One of Britain's largest counties, once made up of separate regions known as the Ridings, Yorkshire is still often divided into North, South, East and West Yorkshire by locals to best describe the character of the areas. Just half an hour's drive or so east of Kendal, along the A68, brings one to the Yorkshire Dales National Park, an agricultural region of vales and dales, dotted with lovely towns and villages, and made famous by James Herriot's semi-autobiographical books about the life of a country vet in *All Creatures Great and Small*. Perennially popular with walkers, the region's most significant town is Richmond, with its impressive 11th-century castle. One of the most popular areas for hikers is the limestone crags of Malham, but they're not for the inexperienced. East of here, on the North York Moors and south, along the Pennine Way, the landscape becomes more rugged and brooding, as epitomised in Emily Brontë's classic novel *Wuthering Heights* – Brontë herself lived all her life in the parsonage at Haworth, now a centre of literary pilgrimage for many. Two abbeys, **Rievaulx** and **Fountains**, the latter with beautiful landscaped gardens, date from the 12th century and are worth a visit, while the spectacular 18th-century stately home, **Castle Howard**, immortalised in the television adaptation of Evelyn Waugh's *Brideshead Revisted*, is a wonderful display of early Georgian architecture inside and out. All the way over on the east coast are seaside towns such as Whitby and Scarborough, popular in the 19th century as health-restorative resorts, although today both with a somewhat faded grandeur. The city of York is one of the most historic in Britain – the Vikings settled here, calling it Jorvik – and is a year-round tourist draw. Its most famous sight is the vast, Gothic, 13th-century church, the York Minster, with its tall towers and stained-glass windows. But history is apparent throughout the city, in the tiny medieval lanes, many of which are now occupied by elegant shops and boutiques. Other popular sights are the **Jorvik Viking Centre**, which recreates the city of the 9th-century with great imagination and attention to detail, and the **National Railway Museum**, detailing the history of rail travel in Britain with a wonderful collection of old trains.

Rievaulx Abbey: 3km (2 miles) from Helmsley. Tel: (01439) 798228. Open: Apr–Sept daily 10am–6pm; Oct Thur–Mon 10am–5pm; Nov–Mar Thur–Mon 10am–4pm. Admission charge.

Fountains Abbey: Studely Royal Estate, Ripon. Tel: (01765) 608888. www.fountainsabbey.org.uk. Open: Mar–Oct daily 10am–5pm; Nov–Feb daily 10am–4pm. Admission charge. Castle Howard: 24km (15 miles) from York. Tel: (01653) 648644. www.castlehoward.co.uk. Open: Mar–Oct & Dec daily 11am–4pm. Admission charge.

Jorvik Viking Centre: Coppergate, York. Tel: (01904) 543400. www.jorvik-viking-centre.co.uk. Open: daily 10am–4pm. Admission charge.

National Railway Museum: Leeman Rd, York. Tel: (08448) 153139. www.nrm.org.uk. Open: daily 10am–6pm. Free admission.

The main street of Haworth in North Yorkshire

When to go

As an area of outstanding natural beauty, the Lake District is a wonderful place to visit in any season. However, whatever the time of year, waterproof clothing, sturdy footwear that can cope with hilly and regularly muddy and slippery slopes are essential, as is an added warm layer, such as a fleece, which could be needed morning and evening, even at the height of summer.

It may seem obvious that the best time to visit the Lake District, climate-wise, is the summer months of June to August. Certainly this period will see the warmest days and least risk of rain (although it's generally a given that a wholly cloud-free trip is unlikely at any time), but you will also be sharing the area with vast numbers of other people from all over the world as well as Britain, and it isn't the best way to appreciate the beauty and tranquillity that the Lakes offer. Accommodation, from hotels to caravans to campsites, will also be booked up far in advance and at higher prices. It is far better to aim for spring (when you will have the added benefit of wildflowers) and early autumn, when crowds have generally dispersed and other visitors are likely to be on the same quest for peaceful exploring, rather than battling queues and traffic jams. Other obvious high periods to avoid if possible are Easter, Christmas and New Year.

Winter is long, dark and wet in Cumbria, so if you hope for much outdoor activity this season should be avoided – that said, wintertime in front of a cosy fire in many of the region's traditional pubs makes for a wonderfully romantic break.

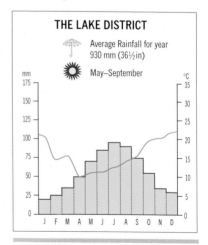

THE LAKE DISTRICT

Average Rainfall for year 930 mm (36½ in)

May–September

WEATHER CONVERSION CHART

25.4mm = 1 inch

°F = 1.8 × °C + 32

It's best to be prepared for some rain

Getting around

If you plan to visit a large proportion of the Lake District and Cumbria, the most obvious solution to getting around is by car, which gives all the independence of being able to go places where and when you want. That said, the roads can be extremely crowded in high season and the region's public transport is very good, recognising the need to cater for the large number of visitors. Tourist offices offer a free book of timetables and other information regarding public transport, including a detailed map.

Bicycle

Mountain biking is very popular in the hills and fells of the Lake District and there are a large number of designated cycle routes that have been planned so that they don't interfere with hiking routes. For more information about each of the trails visit *www.mountain-bike-cumbria.co.uk*

Bus

In an effort to encourage visitors on to public transport and away from private cars, Cumbria has done more than almost any other area of Britain to provide a comprehensive and reliable bus service. Not only is it a cost-effective way to get around, it also allows you to get up close and personal with the passing landscapes without having to concentrate on the road. Even the smallest of villages will have at least one bus service running through it, but the main hubs are the larger towns such as Windermere, Keswick, Cockermouth and Carlisle, from which faster services with

fewer stops can be taken. Tickets are generally bought directly from the driver as you board the bus. Timetables are available at bus stations and bus stops, and main route timetables can also be seen online (*www.stagecoachbus.com*). If you're short of time, an escorted bus tour can be a good option – details are available at tourist offices.

Car

The only motorway that runs through Cumbria is the M6, which follows a route from Rugby to Carlisle. The rest of the region is served by A and B roads, although, given the mountainous landscape, few of the A roads are dual carriageway. For this reason, in high season, traffic can be a serious headache and in the main towns and at popular sights parking is also an issue. Free parking is rare – major sights and destinations have pay and display car parks and all the major towns now operate a parking scheme that requires a disc bought from local newsagents to

Ideal country for mountain biking

be displayed on your car before you are allowed to park anywhere.

Car hire

Car hire firms can be found in Kendal, Penrith, Windermere, Keswick and Carlisle. Details are available in the local telephone directories or from tourist offices.

Emergency

If you are a member of the **AA** (*Tel: 0870 600 0371*) or the **RAC** (*Tel: 0800 197 7815*) or one of their affiliates, you will be able to receive roadside assistance in the event of a breakdown. In the event of an accident or emergency, dial 999. There are emergency telephones along the M6 motorway.

Fuel

Petrol stations, supplying unleaded and diesel, can be found in towns and cities, and there are 24-hour service stations on the M6 motorway.

Insurance

Third Party Insurance is the minimum car insurance that is required in the UK – this covers drivers for injury or damage to another person or vehicle. Third Party, Fire and Theft is the next step up and covers you for exactly what it says; Fully Comprehensive also covers any accidental damage to the car, such as a broken wing mirror or a slashed tyre.

Speed limits

Speed limits in the UK are 50km/h (30mph) in any built up area (towns

A more restful way to travel, here on Coniston Water

and villages), 85km/h (60mph) on single carriageway routes and 110 km/h (70mph) on dual carriageways and motorways. Speed limits are strictly enforced and many roads are fitted with speed cameras that will identify the number plate of any vehicle exceeding the limits, thus ensuring a fine, or even a prosecution.

Taxi

Taxi companies can be found in all the main towns in the region. Details can be obtained from local telephone directories.

Train

The main railway line that runs through Cumbria is the west coast main line from London to Glasgow, which stops at Penrith and Carlisle. There's also a main line that runs from Carlisle to Newcastle on the east coast. The West Cumbrian Line is extremely useful if you want to explore the various coastal towns on the west coast – it runs from Carlisle to Barrow and passes through towns such as Maryport, Whitehaven and Ravenglass (*see pp114–15*). Within the national park itself there is the Lakes Line from Oxenholme to Windermere, via Kendal. The region, however, is the best in the country for its preserved steam railways, and a chance to ride on one of these remnants of the past – such as the Lakeside and Haverthwaite (*see p93*) or Ravenglass and Eskdale (*see p105*) – shouldn't be missed.

There are three rail passes that cover the area, which are useful if you plan to get around predominantly by train – the Cumbrian Coast Day Ranger, the Cumbria Round Robin and the Lakes Day Ranger, the latter available as an individual or family pass. These are available at station ticket offices and further details can be obtained from **National Rail** (*Tel: 08457 484950, www.nationalrail.co.uk*).

Travellers with disabilities

Main line trains do provide limited facilities for wheelchair users but these need to be booked in advance for both the seat on board the train and the ramp used to facilitate boarding. Contact National Rail (*Tel: 08457 484950, www.nationalrail.co.uk*) for more information. Modern buses are now generally designed to enable wheelchair user access, but be aware that in more rural communities this may not be the case. If you have a Blue Badge issued in the UK, if it is prominently displayed in your car window you are entitled to park in designated parking places for free. Many other international badge schemes are also acceptable in the UK but it can vary from country to country so it is best to take the relevant badge to a tourist office or council building to check whether it will be recognised in Great Britain.

Accommodation

There is a wide range of accommodation in the Lake District and, refreshingly enough, there are few large, impersonal chain hotels. Instead there is an enormous amount of privately run hotels and guesthouses, often in charming houses or cottages, set in beautiful grounds, which offer a memorable experience.

Farm stays are another way to turn your accommodation into an extra part of your holiday. Booking ahead is always recommended but is absolutely essential in the summer months and over Christmas and New Year, or you could find yourself experiencing rather more of the great outdoors than you intended. Tourist offices locally will be able to provide a list of accommodation, or contact **Cumbria Tourism** (*Tel: 0845 450 1199, www.golakes.co.uk*) who, for a small fee, can arrange bookings. Visa and Mastercard are the most commonly accepted credit cards for payment – smaller establishments generally don't accept American Express because of the commission they would have to pay. For a list of recommended places to stay in all categories see pp158–73.

Camping

Not surprisingly in this outdoor environment, Cumbria abounds with campsites. These range from caravan sites with static caravans available to rent, sites with pitches with electricity hook-ups and washing facilities, to basic fields rented out by local farms for tent pitches or barns (bunkhouses) offering mattresses. Many of the larger sites also have children's facilities, such as adventure playgrounds or other sports, and some also feature a bar or basic dining options. Despite what may seem like miles and miles of landscape belonging to no one, it is not permissible to pitch a tent in an 'empty' field. For more information about all the campsites available in Cumbria, visit *www.lakedistrictcamping.co.uk*, or for bunkhouses *www. lakelandcampingbarns.co.uk*

Farm stays

Cumbria may still be a largely agricultural region, but British farmers have long struggled financially and the introduction of farm stays, offering visitors bed and breakfast accommodation either within the farmhouse or in neighbouring buildings, has been a boost to many farmers' livelihoods. For the visitor, it also offers a unique experience of genuine day-to-day country life, and the possibility to join in some of the farming activities (particularly charming during the lambing season in spring). Accommodation is likely to be a little bit more basic than in guesthouses, although some do have en suite facilities and in-room TVs. Details of the all the farm stays available in Cumbria can be found at **Farm Stays UK** (*Tel: 024 7669 6909, www.farmstaysuk.co.uk*), who will be able to send you a brochure of their properties. For a combination of 5-star luxury, country living and farm life, however, which really must be the best of all worlds, visit *www.luxuryinafarm.co.uk* for a list of their Cumbrian properties.

Guesthouses and B&Bs

This has long been a boom industry in the Lake District and there is absolutely no shortage of guesthouses or bed and breakfasts, many of which are privately run. The advantage of these over hotels is a more personal service (many of them only have two or three guest rooms), an intimate atmosphere and

There are plenty of B&Bs in the Lake District, such as these in Keswick

staff who are readily available to offer guidance and information on the area. Many are also set within traditional inns or country houses, some dating as far back as the 16th century, adding a touch of history to your stay. Bed and breakfasts are just that, but many of the guesthouses also have a bar area and, on occasion, a small restaurant serving dinner. Most guesthouses these days offer en-suite accommodation but some of the smaller establishments may only offer communal facilities.

Hostels

The Youth Hostel Association has converted a number of properties, many of which have stunning lakeside or wooded locations, into hostel accommodation, and the majority of these offer private or family rooms, although some do have dormitory rooms. Despite the name, there is no age restriction for staying at the hostels. Facilities are generally clean and tidy but with no mod cons, and few offer en suite rooms, but it's an incredibly cost-effective way to solve accommodation issues in an area that can otherwise be expensive.

Hotels

Most of the hotels in the Lake District have recently gone down the 'luxury' route, with many of them offering spa facilities, gyms, swimming pools or similar touches to provide visitors with a relaxing experience. The most popular hotels are obviously those on the edges of lakes or with stunning mountain views, and you will pay for these advantages, but location is all in such a landscape. Many, particularly the 4- and 5-star hotels, are located within converted mansions or stately homes, retaining original architectural features and nice touches such as log fires in winter.

Self-catering

Self-catering accommodation allows a greater sense of independence as well as a more budget-friendly option and is particularly good for holidaying families. The Lake District is dotted all over with cottages that have been converted into self-catering holiday homes, and range from small, picture postcard one-bedroom houses to renovated barns, farmhouses or halls that can accommodate up to 20 people – ideal for group trips. Supermarkets for all groceries can be found in the main towns, but even smaller villages will have a shop selling basic provisions such as milk or bread and some tinned goods. Many of the properties also supply bed linen, but it's worth checking in advance, and some also offer 'welcome' packs of standard groceries such as tea and coffee. Note that in high season many will require a minimum of a one-week stay. There are numerous companies that list properties around the Lakes and Cumbria, as any Internet search will reveal, but **Cumbria Tourism** is probably best starting point (*www.golakes.co.uk*).

A typical hotel, here in Bowness-on-Windermere

Food and drink

British food has never enjoyed much of an international reputation, which is slightly unjust given the wide range of regional specialities that have been produced in different counties for centuries. Drink, however, is always a hot topic – Britain retains a pub culture and arguably produces some of the best beers in the world.

Cumbrian cuisine may be largely meat-based but restaurants are well aware of the need to cater to vegetarians, and most menus will include at least one meat-free dish that is far superior to simply a bland omelette or salad.

Buying food and drink

Many of Cumbria's towns still hold a Saturday food market (and some on Wednesdays, too), which generally sell fresh fruit and vegetables but also offer local specialities produced by nearby farms, such as chutneys, cheese and bread. Local butcher shops, many of which are specialists in producing Cumberland sausage, ham and black pudding, are a good source of quality meats, and a number of independent bakeries sell freshly baked local breads such as whig, flavoured with caraway seeds.

Regional specialities

The two best-known culinary specialities of the Lake District are Cumberland

sausage and Kendal Mint Cake. The former is a long pork sausage, often sold by length rather than weight, spiced with herbs and pepper, and generally sold and cooked curved in coil-like shape. The latter is a rather sickly brittle mint-flavoured sweet that has a reputation for sustaining walkers on long hikes among the fells – a belief that began when Sir Edmund Hillary took Kendal Mintcake with him on his 1953 Everest expedition.

With its abundance of sheep farms, lamb is the most popular meat in Cumbria and is used in dishes such as cottage pie (minced lamb mixed with tomatoes, onion and carrots and topped

Local chutney for sale

with mashed potato) and tattie pot, a similar dish that also includes swede and black pudding. Cumberland ham is a dry-cured ham with sugar coating, while Cumberland sauce, made from redcurrant jelly, mustard, port, ginger and orange and lemon juice is a great accompaniment. Cumberland rum butter is a traditional accompaniment to Christmas pudding. In terms of fish, lake-caught trout and Arctic char are the most common. There are a number of local apple varieties, but the most abundant local fruit is damson, commonly used in chutney. For those with a sweet tooth, fudge and gingerbread are also local specialities.

Where to eat

There is a wide range of options for eating out in Cumbria. From fine dining, offering silver service and three- or four-course menus, to smaller and less formal independent restaurants, to chain establishments and ethnic offerings (predominantly Chinese and Indian) to fast food and takeaways. Many pubs also serve food, generally simple fare such as steak and kidney pie or fish and chips. The region also has an abundance of tea shops, selling a variety of pastries, which can be charmingly old-fashioned. A lakeside cream tea, consisting of scones served with clotted cream and jam, is a lovely afternoon refreshment.

Tipping

As a general rule, unless service has been particularly bad, a tip of between 10 and 12 per cent should be added to all restaurant bills, but do check the bill first – some restaurants add the tip automatically before bringing you the receipt to sign. Tipping is not required in pubs or bars.

Pubs and bars

Cumbria still has plenty of rural country pubs that make an atmospheric evening out, particularly in front of a roaring fire. In addition there are a number of local breweries that produce top quality ales, such as Jennings, Yates and Coniston Brewing Company. If you're a beer lover and want to find the best pubs in the region for the ales on offer it is worth buying a copy of the Cumbria Real Ale Guide from **CAMRA** (*www.camra.org.uk*).

MICROBREWERIES

The British love for their pint of beer is well and truly thriving in Cumbria, where there are some 16 microbreweries, and growing, producing more than 70 different types of beer. The first to open was Yates Brewery in Westnewton, begun in 1986, but there are now many more that produce award-winning ales. Bluebird bitter, produced by Coniston Brewery, has won the top award from CAMRA (Campaign for Real Ale), which is devoted to preserving authentic and quality beers in Britain. Other local highlights are the wonderfully named Pigs Might Fly beer from the Hesket Newmarket Brewery, the Woolpacker from the Hardknott Brewery in Eskdale, and the Cocker Hoop from Jennings Brewery in Cockermouth.

Entertainment

The focus of any visit to the Lake District has to be the wonder of the countryside, rather than sitting within the confines of a darkened theatre or cinema, so unsurprisingly there is not a wealth of entertainment options here. In summer, however, the region does stage a number of lively festivals (see pp24–5), most of which are outdoors, and these bring a range of arts-based activities to the area.

Cinema

There is a seven-screen cinema at the Rheged Centre in Penrith, showing all the latest releases, but there are a number of other cinemas in towns such as Keswick, Carlisle and Ambleside, where Zeffirelli's also features a restaurant and a jazz bar.

Nightlife

Nobody goes to the Lake District on the premise of finding wild and wacky

The Alhambra Cinema in Keswick opened before World War I

nightlife. The nightclubs here are obviously geared towards local 20-somethings and not big-city ravers, so you can expect small venues, casual dress and music that sticks rather firmly to bouncy chart music rather than more esoteric genres such as trance or trip hop. That said, the atmosphere is generally friendly, entrance charges are low, and they can offer a fun night out if you want to let your hair down. The nightclubs in the region include **CAI** in Carlisle (*17 Botchergate. Tel: 01228 530460*), **Blues Night Club** in Penrith (*Southend Road. Tel: 01768 863212*), **Buffers Club** in Ulverston (*Station Approach. Tel: 01229 586366*), **The Park** in Whitehaven (*Duke Street. Tel: 01946 67773*) and **Fusion Nightclub** in Workington (*Ladies Walk. Tel: 01900 606030*).

Pubs and bars

One of the pleasures of a visit to the Lake District is the large number of

A performance in full swing at the Theatre by the Lake in Keswick

traditional country pubs that still exist in the area, allowing for a cosy pint of beer in the evening after a day in the great outdoors. The area has highly respected breweries of its own, such as **Jennings**, as well as several microbreweries (*see p137*), so the quality and choice of ales available is excellent. There are more details on recommended pubs and inns in the area in the Directory section (*see pp158–73*), but if you're looking for a more modern and trendy experience, there are options in the area's main towns.

Try **Lake Road Wine Bar** (*12–14 Lake Road. Tel: 08715 297819*) or **Lucy4 Wine Bar** (*St Mary's Lane. Tel: 08718 114669*) in Ambleside, or **Café Bar 26** in Keswick (*26 Lake Road. Tel: 01768 780863*).

Theatre

The best-known and most popular theatrical experience in the Lakes is the **Theatre by the Lake** in Keswick, which stages a varied programme year-round (*www.theatrebythelake.com*) including a number of festivals (*see pp24–5*). Another popular theatre is the **Rosehill Theatre** in Whitehaven, on the west coast (*www.rosehilltheatre.co.uk*). Lakes Leisure Kendal is an entertainment centre that stages drama, stand-up comedy, and classical and popular music concerts. Forum Twenty Eight, in Barrow-in-Furness, and Millom Palladium, in Millom, are the two other main performance venues in the region. The Canteen Comedy Club, also in Barrow-in-Furness, stages a year-round programme of local and national comedy talent.

Shopping

The most obvious souvenirs of any trip to the Lake District are some of the many local food products on offer (see pp136–7), as well as local crafts. Landscape paintings of the area are also a popular memento.

All the major towns and cities have shopping areas with standard chain stores as well as some individual boutiques and shops. Given that this is an area that attracts outdoor sports enthusiasts year-round, it's also a great place to find outdoor clothing and accessory outlets. Museum shops are also always a good bet for souvenirs relating to aspects of the area, such as Beatrix Potter memorabilia (*see p50*), poetry books by the Lake Poets (*see p34*), or even more quirky items such as pencils from the Cumberland Pencil Museum (*see p35*).

Arts and crafts

The **Lakeland Sheep and Wool Visitors Centre** not only sells a variety of woollen items, from gifts to clothing, it's also a great day out to learn about sheep farming in the region (*Egremont Road, Cockermouth. Tel: 01900 822673*). As well as its farm shop, Low Sizergh Barn has a crafts shop stocking local knitwear, pottery, glassworks, basketry,

handmade cards and more. Glass-blowing is a very traditional Cumbrian craft and there are two excellent centres where lights, bowls, glasses and more can be purchased – **Adrian Sankey Glass Makers** (*Rydal Road, Ambleside. Tel: 015394 31139. www.glassmakers.co.uk*) and the **Lakes Glass Centre** on the A590 road near Ulverston (*Tel: 01229 581385*). Two of the best places to purchase a quality landscape painting of the Lakes are at the **William Heaton Cooper Gallery** in Grasmere (*Tel: 015394 35280. www.heatoncooper.co.uk*), established by the renowned local artist and now run by his son, and **Slapestones Gallery** (*Pye Lane, Grasmere. Tel: 01539 35252. www.slapestonesgallery.co.uk*), which sells beautifully atmospheric watercolours of the area. Lovely ceramics by local potter Gordon Fox are available at **Kentmere Pottery** near Kendal (*Tel: 01539 821621. www.kentmerepottery.co.uk*), but for something even more quirky and fun,

Glass made by hand at the Lakes Glass Centre in Ulverston

try **The Teapottery** (*4 Packhorse Court, Keswick. Tel: 01768 773983. www.teapottery.co.uk*), where teapots have been fashioned to resemble all manner of objects, such as a classic campervan caravan, a jar of Marmite, a piano, and even a computer. You can send them ideas if you want your own personalised teapot designed.

Local produce

Cumberland sausage (*see p136*) can be found in butchers all over the region, but the general consensus is that the best is available from **Richard Woodall** in Waberthwaite, near Millom (*Lane End, Waberthwaite. Tel: 01229 717237. www.richardwoodall.co.uk*), which also sells excellent Cumberland ham. They also have an online shop if you want to order more sausages or ham once you

get home. The original home of Kendal Mint Cake is **Romney's** in Kendal (*Mintsfeet Trading Estate, Kendal. Tel: 01539 720155. www.kendal. mintcake.co.uk*), but it can be found in sweet shops around the region.

Cranstons Cumbrian Food Hall in Penrith (*Ullswater Road. Tel: 01768 868680*) is a great all-round shop for all local Cumbrian food stuffs, while **Hawkshead Relish Company** is a treasure trove of locally made relishes and chutneys, with tastings available before you buy (*2 The Square, Hawkshead, Ambleside. Tel: 01539 436614*). Sarah Nelson's gingerbread is considered the best in the county and can be bought at the **Grasmere Gingerbread Shop** (*Church Cottage, Grasmere. Tel: 01539 435428*). Of all the local breweries **Jennings** is the most

Tempting home-made pies on sale

symbolic of the region. Tours of the brewery can be taken, and there's a shop where you can buy any of their many varieties of ale (*Castle Brewery, Cockermouth. Tel: 0845 1297190*). The **Cartmel Village Shop** is also something of a local legend; best known for supposedly being the birthplace of sticky toffee pudding, it's also an emporium stocking the best of Cumbrian produce, including cheeses, breads, jams and beers (*Parkgate House, The Square, Cartmel. Tel: 015395 36280*). The farm shop at **Low Sizergh Barn** is also a fantastic resource for all locally produced foods from nearby farms (*Low Sizergh Farm, Sizergh, Kendal. Tel: 015395 60426. www.lowsizerghbarn. co.uk*). If you visit in the afternoon you can even watch the cows being milked as you enjoy a cup of tea and a slice of cake in the tearoom.

Outdoor equipment

The most renowned outdoor clothing and accessory store in the Lake District is **George Fisher** (*2 Borrowdale Road, Keswick. Tel: 017687 72178. www.georgefisheronline.co.uk*). This huge store supplies everything you could need for hiking, camping and other outdoor activities, including expert boot-fitting services, fleeces, sleeping bags and tents, maps and navigation equipment and rucksacks. They also run navigation courses and other activities, if booked in advance. Keen fishermen should also head to the **Angling and Hiking Centre** (*275 Rawlinson Street, Barrow-in-Furness. Tel: 01229 829661. www. anglingandhikingcentre.co.uk*) for rods, bait and more. They also have a large supply of outdoor equipment, including walking boots by well-known names, rucksacks, and a variety of climbing and navigation equipment.

Shopping areas

The centres of all the main towns – Carlisle, Kendal, Keswick, Penrith, Cockermouth and Ambleside – have shopping areas that include all the usual chain stores found in the rest of the UK, such as Boots, WHSmith, Marks and Spencer, H&M and Next. Kendal also has an outlet centre, **K Village** (*20 Stricklandgate, Kendal. Tel: 01539 732373*) where retailers such as the National Trust and Clarks sell products at greatly reduced prices. There is also a House of Fraser department store in Carlisle, for clothes, cosmetics, electrical equipment and more, all under one roof.

Tax-free shopping

If any shop displays a Tax-free Shopping sign in their window, residents from outside the European Union are entitled to claim back the VAT on their purchase. A form should be obtained from the shop when making the purchase and this must be completed by both the store and the buyer, before being presented to customs at the airport when leaving the UK.

Sport and leisure

For those with a passion for the outdoors, there can be few better areas in England than the Lake District. A vast array of sports is available, from the most obvious of hiking on the fells, to messing about in boats on the lakes themselves, to more extreme offerings such as caving and hang-gliding. It's also a beautiful landscape to explore astride either a mountain bike or a horse, or take it all in from the air in a memorable hot-air balloon trip. If pampering is what you're after, there is an increasing number of spas in the region.

Angling

Not surprisingly, given the amount of water in the region, the Lake District is an extremely popular destination for anglers, and its lakes are abundant for those who enjoy game fishing.

The predominant species in the area is trout, with rainbow, brown and ferox inhabiting the waters, but there are also some populations of chub, roach, grayling and salmon. For those who enjoy coarse fishing, large pike, carp and bream can also be found in some areas.

The main trout-fishing season is between June and September. Wild trout are becoming increasingly rare so the general rule is that any catch should

A peaceful spot to fish overlooking Skiddaw

be returned to the water unharmed. In many of the lakes, including Coniston, Bassenthwaite, Ennerdale, Ullswater and Windermere, the use of live or dead freshwater fish as bait is strictly prohibited, as is the use of lead weights, and fines are high and heavily enforced. Artificial bait, or dead sea fish, however, are acceptable.

Anglers should be properly equipped before embarking on any activity, including fishing. Detailed maps (the best available are Ordnance Survey maps), a compass and a fully charged mobile phone are recommended, aside from the usual waterproof gear. Some waters, such as Windermere, also require a rod licence and fishing permits available from the environment agency (*www.environment-agency.gov.uk*).

Caving

For those who love to scramble down beneath the ground and explore networks of narrow, damp stone corridors, the caves near Kirkby Lonsdale are the most popular, but the region's mining history has also left many abandoned mine sites ready for exploration. This is not a sport to be undertaken by the inexperienced individual – qualified leaders are required.

Cycling and mountain biking

There are hundreds of designated cycle paths in Cumbria that offer a full-on escape from motorists, and a number of organised long-distance routes such as the Cumbria Cycle Way, around the whole county, and the C2C route, from Whitehaven to the east coast in Sunderland (*www.c2c-guide.co.uk*). There's also Hadrian's Cycleway, following the full course along Hadrian's Wall (*see pp60–61*), and the Reivers Cycle Route from Whitehaven to Bewcastle, along the English-Scottish border (*www.reivers-guide.co.uk*).

For the fitter and more adventurous, the mountain landscape offers some of the best terrain for mountain biking, with steep and strenuous ascents followed by some jaw-dropping descents (*see pp162 & 171*).

Golf

True golfing enthusiasts should really head over the border to Scotland – the birthplace of the sport – as Cumbria is not renowned for its facilities. That said, there are a total of 32 courses, most of which charge a day or weekend rate (*see pp162 & 173*).

Hang-gliding and paragliding

In good weather, look up at the sky and you are more than likely to see daredevils launching themselves off mountaintops attached only to a harness and a steel frame covered with a canopy. Few areas of Britain are better designed for hang-gliding and there are a number of operators who can offer instruction.

Paragliding is similar to parachuting, except it involves jumping off the edge of a mountain instead of out of a plane, but if you have the nerve it's a wonderful way to glide slowly and

Hikers stop and admire the view in Great Langdale

tranquilly over the landscape and back down to earth. Instruction is absolutely essential and beginners start with a tandem flight, taking the leap alongside a qualified teacher (*see p167*).

Hiking and walking

The most obvious and popular sports in the Lake District are walking and hiking among the many fells and mountains that make up this spectacular landscape. On any given day, even in pouring rain, you are likely to see armies of people in sturdy walking boots and lightweight rain gear gamely going up and down the hills, stopping only to take in the magnificent views. Many follow designated routes, such as those made popular by Alfred Wainwright (*see p54*),

and often spend days or weeks following long distance routes such as the Cumbria Way or the Cumbria Coastal Way. Many also come back year after year to discover yet another pocket of the region. But there's no necessity in doing so and no instruction is needed – just follow your nose and it's a given that you'll find beauty at every turn. Just make sure you follow the safety guidelines listed below. If you prefer to remain on the flat there are still memorable walks such as along Hadrian's Wall, or the Eden or Eskdale valleys. There is also a vast number of companies that offer guided walks in the region, from day hikes to week-long trips, staying either at hostels or campsites overnight (*see p171*).

Horse riding

As with cycling, exploring the Lake District on horseback is an exhilarating way to get around, allowing access across fells, and through woodlands and forests that would otherwise be off limits. Horse riding centres offer trails for both beginners and experienced equestrians, and a range of treks, ranging from a couple of hours to several days (*see pp167 & 171*).

Hot air ballooning

A truly unforgettable experience is to climb aboard the basket of a hot air balloon, hear the whoosh of the balloon inflating, then take off with the wind, across the lakes, fields and farmsteads below. As if that wasn't special enough, a glass of champagne can be enjoyed by all on landing. For details of hot air ballooning operators see p162.

Rock climbing

Cumbria is the birthplace of rock climbing as a sport, and the native limestone, sandstone and gritstone crags still offer the best opportunities in England for climbing enthusiasts – particularly in the Northern Fells. If you are experienced and have all the right equipment, there's no reason why you can't take off alone to scramble up or abseil down the main peaks. But there are plenty of operators that can offer

Canoeing on Ullswater

training to beginners, both outdoors and on indoor climbing walls, and they also offer guided climbs (*see pp167, 171 & 173*).

Spas

Spas and leisure centres are booming across Britain and Cumbria is no exception. Either in designated facilities or in top-end hotels, such as the Lakeside Hotel in Windermere (*see p159*), treatments such as massage, reflexology, facials and aromatherapy are all available to make visitors feel both healthy and pampered. Most centres will also have an indoor swimming pool, sauna and steam room.

Watersports

As one would assume from a name like the Lake District, there is literally no end to the watersports facilities and possibilities in the area.

Canoeing and kayaking

Canoeing is one of the most straightforward, and therefore accessible and enjoyable sports to undertake on the lakes. Vessels can be hired for independent activities, or guided canoe trips can be booked with operators. Kayaking is a slightly tougher option, riding fast-flowing streams, but is an exhilarating experience where you really feel at one with the landscape. Again, instruction and equipment hire are readily available at designated centres (*see pp162, 171 & 173*).

Sailing

The most obvious sport here is to take to the water in any number of sailing vessels available to hire around the Lakes. From dinghies to yachts, even a Viking longship on Derwentwater, nothing beats exploring the region from the viewpoint that has made it so famous. On smaller vessels, instruction is not necessary, but lessons are available from a number of operators if required (*see p162*). Alternatively, leave the calm waters of the lakes behind and head to the coast at Whitehaven to experience the slightly choppier waters of the Solway Firth.

Water skiing

With the reduction of the speed limit that boats are allowed to travel on the lakes (*see p12*), water skiing has taken a bit of a bashing of late. But 16km/h (10mph) is quite fast enough if you're a novice at the sport and there are instructors available at Windermere (*see p40*). Water skiing is also available off the west coast.

CUMBRIAN WRESTLING

Many areas of Britain have retained traditional sports whose origins have been lost in the mists of time, and Cumbrian wrestling remains a popular activity at local summer fairs. Possibly dating from the Viking era, the sport involves two men gripping each other with their right arms and chins and then trying to bring the other to the ground or break their partner's hold. Also in keeping with tradition, the wrestlers are only permitted to wear vest tops and stockings.

A Cumbrian wrestler takes on a Scottish opponent at Grasmere

Wind surfing

The resorts of the west coast are very popular with windsurfers, providing ideal climatic conditions for quite a challenging day out. The calmer waters on the lakes, of course, are ideal for beginners. Several operators offer instruction and equipment.

Safety information

Even if you're only planning a gentle ramble, it's essential to have good quality walking shoes or boots, waterproof and warm clothing (fleeces are lightweight and ideal), a map of the area, a compass, and drinking water with you. Ideally, a fully charged mobile phone is also advisable. The weather is changeable at all times of year in the Lake District so most hotels, realising they are generally catering to hikers, list the forecast each day at reception. Alternatively, the **Lake District National Park Weatherline** (*Tel: 0870 055 0575*) provides up-to-date information. If you are planning a relatively long hike, it's also advisable to inform your hotel, guesthouse, or hostel where you are planning to go.

Children

The Lake District is a fantastic destination for a family holiday, with a vast range of outdoor activities. Even on a rainy day there are plenty of attractions that will delight young ones, from all the Beatrix Potter-related attractions, to unique examples such as the Cumberland Pencil Museum (see p35) or a ride on one of the steam trains (see pp84, 93 & 105). It's a child-friendly destination – many hotels offer family rooms, and restaurants will either have a children's menu or will be happy to serve smaller portions.

Animal attractions

Ducky's Park Farm

Entirely designed to appeal to children is this petting farm, home to goats, sheep, pigs, alpacas and the eponymous Dilly the Duck. Children can get up close and personal with the animals, help in the feeding and even be an animal keeper for a day, if booked in advance. There is also an indoor and outdoor playground to keep them amused.
Moor Lane, Flookburgh, Grange-over-Sands. Tel: 01539 559293.
www.duckysparkfarm.co.uk.
Open: Apr–Sept daily 10.30am–5pm.
Admission charge.

Eden Ostrich World

A working farm best known for its black ostriches, but also full of horses, sheep and pigs, as well as a zebroid – a cross between a zebra and a horse. There's also an adventure playground, a maze, tractor rides and indoor playground. Should keep children of all ages amused all day.

Langwathby Hall Farm, Langwathby, Penrith. Tel: 01768 881771.
www.ostrich-world.com. Open: Feb–Oct daily 10am–5pm; Nov–Jan Wed–Mon 10am–5pm. Admission charge.

High Hall Nursery

Equally enjoyable for adults, this woodland walk has taken children into consideration by lining the route with 'homes' of woodland animals such as Sebastian Shrew and Montague Mouse. Squirrels and deer can also be spotted along the walk as well as many varieties of birdlife.
Westward, Wigton. Tel: 01697 344308.
www.highhallnursery.co.uk.
Open: mid-Apr–mid-Oct Fri–Sun 10am–4pm. Free admission.

Leighton Moss Nature Reserve

Run by the Royal Society for the Protection of Birds, avocets, bitterns and marsh harriers are just some of the rare species that are protected in this reedbed area. There's a nature trail to follow and a Visitor Centre that explains many of the birds that can be spotted. There's also a calendar of guided walks following different themes.

Myers Farm, Silverdale, Carnforth. Tel: 01524 701601. Open: Feb–Oct daily 9.30am–5pm; Nov–Jan daily 9.30am–4.30pm. Admission charge.

South Lakes Wild Animal Park

A zoo-cum-park with a strong emphasis on conservation, the real highlight here is being able to hand-feed many of the animals, including penguins, giraffes and kangaroos (under supervised guidance). Other animals included in the park are lions, tigers, rhinos, lemurs and plenty more.

Broughton Road, Dalton-in-Furness. Tel: 01229 466086. www.wildanimalpark.co.uk. Open: Mar–Sept daily 10am–5pm. Admission charge.

Trotters World of Animals

Another animal park with a varied range of inhabitants, from a Canadian lynx to wild boar, to zebra and marmosets. There's a strong emphasis on educating children about animal and environmental conservation, but there are plenty of play areas to keep the younger ones amused.

Coalbeck Farm, Bassenthwaite. Tel: 01768 776239. www.trottersworld.com. Open: daily 10am–dusk. Admission charge.

Children

Giraffes at South Lakes Wild Animal Park

Essentials

Arriving and departing
By air
The nearest international airports to Cumbria can be found at Glasgow, Newcastle, Leeds Bradford and Blackpool (the latter covering destinations in Europe only).

By rail
The west coast main line that runs from London Kings Cross to Glasgow, in Scotland, stops at both Penrith and Carlisle en route. There is also a direct rail line between Newcastle and Carlisle.

By road
The M6 motorway runs through Cumbria and connects with the M1 at Rugby to London and the M74 at Carlisle to Glasgow. The A66, which is dual carriageway for much of the route, provides access from Yorkshire.

Customs
EU residents are not restricted on importing any tobacco or alcohol quantities as long as it can be proven that what is brought to the UK is for personal use and not for resale. Excessive amounts (more than 3,000 cigarettes, or 10 litres of spirits, for example) will raise suspicion and may be confiscated. Visitors from all non-EU countries have the following allowances: 200 cigarettes or 100 cigarillos or 50 cigars or 250g of tobacco; 60cc of perfume; 250 cc of eau de toilette; 2 litres of still table wine; 1 litre of spirits or strong liqueurs over 22 per cent volume or 2 litres of fortified wine, sparkling wine or other liqueurs; £145 worth of all other goods including gifts and souvenirs. All visitors must be 17 or over to bring tobacco or alcohol into the country.

Electricity
Electricity in the UK runs on 220 AC voltage, and sockets require plugs with three square pins. Visitors from overseas will require adaptor plugs, which are best bought in their home country before their trip.

Internet
There are Internet cafés all over the Lake District, and many bars and cafés are now installing wireless connections, which mean that you can surf the net on your own laptop if you are wireless-enabled. The larger hotels (and some of the smaller ones, too) generally offer Internet facilities, as do local libraries.

Money
Currency
The British currency is the pound sterling, with 100 pence to one pound. Coins come in denominations of 1, 2, 5, 10, 20 and 50 pence, and 1 and 2

pound coins. Notes come in denominations of 5, 10, 20 and 50 pound notes. Note that if you are planning to include Scotland in part of your trip, Scottish banknotes, although legal tender in England, are issued by Scottish banks and have a different appearance. If you have any Scottish notes in your possession at the end of your trip it is advisable to exchange them before leaving, as they can be extremely difficult to exchange abroad.

ATMs

ATMs (known as cashpoints in the UK) can be found outside most banks, in shopping centres and on high streets. Most will issue cash to foreign cards with the correct pin as long as one of the symbols (such as Cirrus) on the ATM correspond to the symbol on the card.

Exchange

Bureaux de change can be found at airports, mainline railway stations, in larger post offices and on the high street of major cities. A small percentage charge is usually added to any exchange transaction.

Credit and debit cards

Most hotels, restaurants, larger shops, petrol stations and bars will accept the major credit cards (Mastercard and Visa) – if they don't they usually display this very clearly so you don't get caught out when you come to pay the bill. American Express is generally only accepted in very large establishments. Smaller bed and breakfasts, particularly if they are family run with only a couple of guest rooms, may insist on being paid in cash. UK debit cards are also generally accepted everywhere except in the smallest of shops or guesthouses.

Opening hours

Shops and post offices are usually open from Monday to Saturday 9am to 5pm, although larger places, including supermarkets, may have longer hours and open on Sundays. In small villages, shops and post offices generally close at noon on Wednesdays. Banks are open

A typical signpost in the Lake District

Monday to Friday 9.30am to 3.30pm, with branches in the main cities sometimes open on Saturday mornings as well.

Passports and visas

Visitors from EU countries and Switzerland do not require a visa to enter the UK but must have a valid passport with photo ID. Visitors from the USA, Canada, Australia, New Zealand and South Africa do not need a visa if their stay is under six months. Residents from any other country should check the website *www.ukvisas.gov.uk* to check whether a visa is required.

Pharmacies

Pharmacies can be found in shopping areas of main towns and in chain stores such as Boots. All of them have qualified staff able to treat minor ailments or issue prescriptions. They follow standard shop opening hours but will list late night pharmacies nearby in their window. If you need regular medication it is advised to bring either enough to cover the length of the trip or a prescription from your doctor that lists the generic name, as trade names of medicines can vary from country to country.

Post

Many village post offices have been forced to close in recent years, but any town or city will offer post office services and many villages incorporate these services within the local shop – look for the Royal Mail sign.

Public holidays

1 January – New Year's Day
Good Friday – (late March or early April)
Easter Monday – (late March or early April)
First Monday in May – Bank holiday
Last Monday in May – Bank holiday
Last Monday in August – Bank holiday
25 December – Christmas Day
26 December – Boxing Day

Smoking

Since 2007 smoking has been banned in all public places, which includes restaurants, bars, public transport, stations and airports. Most hotels ban smoking as well, although some have set aside designated smoking rooms, which is legal as a private room is not considered a public place. Smoking is permitted at outside tables.

Suggested reading
Fiction

Beatrix Potter: the charming illustrated tales of Peter Rabbit, Jemima Puddleduck and more are the most famous stories to come out of the Lake District, and still enchant children and adults alike (*see pp22–3*).

Swallows and Amazons (Arthur Ransome). The first in a quintet of tales about children's adventures in the Lakes (*see p41*).

Rogue Herries (Hugh Walpole). First of a quartet of novels that follows the lives and loves of a local family.

The Cumbrian Trilogy (Melvyn Bragg). Another saga of local family life in three parts by the TV broadcaster about his native county.

Non-fiction

Hidden Lives and *Precious Lives* (Margaret Forster). A biographical account of the novelist's own family over three generations in Cumbria.
Strong Lad Wanted for Strong Lass (Hunter Davies). Forster's husband gives an account of his own childhood in Carlisle.
Feet in the Clouds (Richard Askwith). An amusing account of being a devoted fell runner.
A Literary Guide to the Lake District (Grevel Lindop). Book lovers will find this an invaluable guide to the literary heritage of the area.
Unruly Times (AS Byatt). A very readable biography of Wordsworth and Coleridge, and their relationship as friends and poets.

Telephones

Public phone boxes can be found in towns and cities and generally accept either coins or phone cards, which can be purchased in various values at newsagents or post offices. The country code for the UK is *44*. For directory enquiries dial *118 118*. For operator services dial *100*, or *150* for an international operator. To dial abroad from the UK, dial *00* then the country code:
Australia *61*
New Zealand *64*
South Africa *27*
USA and Canada *1*

Mobiles

UK mobile phones use the GSM network, so if your phone does the same and has a roaming facility, you should be able to use your mobile in Britain. Mobile (cell) phones from the USA will not work in the UK. Note that signals in remote areas and on mountains can be poor.

Time

Great Britain is on British Standard Time; the rest of Europe is mostly 1 or 2 hours ahead. Australia and New Zealand are 10 hours ahead; east coast USA and Canada are 5 hours behind; west coast USA and Canada are 8 hours behind; South Africa is 1 hour ahead.

Toilets

Public toilets can be found in railway and bus stations, department stores, shopping centres and major tourist sites, and are free to use and generally of a high standard. Using toilets in restaurants and pubs and bars is restricted to customers only.

Travellers with disabilities

Major advances have been made to make public transport accessible to wheelchair users (*see p131*), and road crossings in major towns and cities are equipped with a beep system to alert those with impaired vision when it is safe to cross. For more information contact **RADAR** (*www.radar.org.uk*), which offers advice on facilities available for disabled travellers.

Emergencies

Medical services

Casualty

There are Accident and Emergency (A&E) departments at:

Westmorland General Hospital *Burton Road, Kendal. Tel: 01539 732288.*

Cumberland Infirmary
Newtown Road, Carlisle.
Tel: 01228 523444.

West Cumberland Hospital
Homewood, Hensingham, Whitehaven.
Tel: 01946 693181.

Furness General Hospital
Dalton Lane, Barrow-in-Furness.
Tel: 01229 870870.

Doctors

General practitioners in the UK operate from surgeries that cater only to their registered patients. However, all the hospitals above as well as smaller hospitals in Keswick, Alston, Brampton, Maryport and Workington have minor injuries units, which generally have far shorter waiting times than casualty departments if your injury is not an emergency. The National Health Service (NHS) also runs a 24-hour telephone service if you want to enquire about any symptoms and advice on what to do (*Tel: 0845 4647. www.nhsdirect.nhs.uk*).

Health insurance

No vaccinations are required to visit the UK. Members of EU countries are entitled to free treatment on the NHS if they are in possession of a European Health Insurance Card (*www.ehic.org.uk*). Residents of all other countries are strongly advised to take out health insurance before travelling as costs of medical treatment can escalate very quickly.

Health risks

There are no specific health risks involved in visiting the Lake District, other than attempting to scale the mountains in inadequate footwear, resulting in sprained ankles or worse. If taking to the hills make sure you follow the safety guidelines on *p149*.

Opticians

High street opticians such as Specsavers or Vision Express can offer eye tests and replacement lenses or glasses.

Crime

Cumbria is one of the safest corners of Britain, although in the crowded summer months and at popular tourist sites, common sense should prevail – keep valuables to a minimum and out of sight, always lock car doors when leaving the vehicle and report any theft or crime-related incident to the police immediately.

Embassies

There are no embassies or consulates in Cumbria itself, but the following embassies and high commissions in London will be able to assist with enquiries:

American Embassy
24 Grosvenor Square, London W1A 2LQ.
Tel: (020) 7499 9000.

Australian High Commission
Strand, London WC2B 4LA.
Tel: (020) 7379 4334.

Canadian High Commission
38 Grosvenor Street,
London W1K 4AA.
Tel: (020) 7258 6600.

New Zealand High Commission
New Zealand House, 80 Haymarket,
London SW1Y 4TQ.
Tel: (020) 7930 8422.

South African High Commission
South Africa House, Trafalgar Square,
London WC2N 5DP.
Tel: (020) 7451 7299.

Emergencies

Taking no chances at Derwentwater

Directory

Accommodation price guide

Accommodation ratings are based on a double room for one
night with two people sharing, on a bed and breakfast basis
(unless otherwise stated).

★	under £50
★★	£51–£70
★★★	£71–£100
★★★★	over £100

Eating out price guide

Eating out ratings are based on a three-course meal for one
from the à la carte menu, without drinks.

★	under £15
★★	£15–£25
★★★	£25–£40
★★★★	above £40

LAKE DISTRICT NATIONAL PARK

ACCOMMODATION

Hill of Oaks Caravan Park ★

In the grounds of a working farm, in woodland right on the shore of the lake, this is one of the most attractive campsites in the whole of the Lake District. There are 43 caravan pitches – but no tent pitches. Fishing, sailing and other watersports are available.
Newby Bridge Road, Windermere.
Tel: 01539 531578.
www.hillofoaks.co.uk

Kings Arms Hotel ★

A very good budget option in a central location. This 17th-century coaching inn is still taking in travellers in its 13 traditionally decorated rooms, and there is an on-site restaurant, bar and pizzeria.
Main Street, Keswick.
Tel: 01768 772083

The Queens Hotel ★

The décor, particularly in the bedrooms, may be a little bit old-fashioned, but that's a small price to pay for being right in the centre of the pretty market town of Keswick (*see pp34–7*) and at budget prices. There's no restaurant but light meals are served in either of the two on-site bars and, as a nod to modernity, the hotel is equipped with wireless broadband throughout.
Main Street, Keswick.
Tel: 01768 773333.
www.queenshotel.co.uk

Dale Head Hall Lakeside Hotel ★★

There are views of Helvellyn (*see p75*) from this converted 16th-century house set in beautiful grounds on the banks of Thirlmere, which itself offers plenty of fishing opportunities. There are also self-catering options in designated cottages on the grounds.
Thirlmere, Keswick.
Tel: 01768 772478.
www.daleheadhall.co.uk

Derwent Lodge Hotel ★★

One of the many Georgian properties in

the area that have now been converted into hotels, this one offers wonderful views over Derwentwater. One room features a stunning four-poster bed and all rooms offer TVs and free broadband facilities.
Portinscale, Keswick.
Tel: 01768 773145.
www.derwentlodgehotel.co.uk

Grove Cottages ★★
Four individual cottages on farm grounds offer wonderful self-catering accommodation with views of both Windermere and The Old Man of Coniston from their windows. Original stonework and beams have been left in place but combined with light and airy modern furnishings. The cottages accommodate between two and six people.
Grove Farm, Stockghyll Lane, Ambleside.
Tel: 01539 433074.
www.grovecottages.com

Ravenstone Hotel ★★
The exterior may retain its lovely Victorian façade but the bedrooms in this friendly hotel, just outside Keswick, are decorated in an elegantly understated but modern manner. There's also a 'spa' room that includes an en-suite jacuzzi. The restaurant serves a four-course fixed price menu that tries to make the best of local, seasonal produce.
Bassenthwaite.
Tel: 0800 163983. www.ravenstone-hotel.co.uk

Waterside Hotel ★★
As its name suggests, this country house hotel is on the banks of the lake and set within lovely grounds. The 82 rooms are decorated in a traditional manner (cushions, velvet, chintz) but are equipped with satellite TV and tea- and coffee-making facilities. Good value for money, given its location.
Keswick Road, Grasmere.
Tel: 0870 3339135. www.watersidegrasmere.com

Armathwaite Hall Hotel ★★★
Set in a stately home that is still lived in and run by one family, this is a stunning location on the banks of Bassenthwaite Lake and with vast grounds where roaming deer can regularly be seen. The interior includes an oak-panelled lounge, bedrooms with four-poster canopied beds and a modern indoor swimming pool. The award-winning restaurant combines French and British cuisine whilst priding itself on using plenty of local and seasonal produce.
Bassenthwaite, Keswick.
Tel: 01768 776551. www.armathwaite-hall.com

Lakeside Hotel ★★★
Considered one of the best hotels in the Lake District, this 4-star establishment combines the traditional (oak panelling, cosy bar) with the modern (conservatory with lake views and a large indoor pool and spa centre). The 77 rooms vary in style, from suites to rooms with jacuzzis or family rooms. If you prefer large-scale accommodation to more intimate guesthouses, this is for you.
Newby Bridge.
Tel: 01539 530001.
www.lakesidehotel.co.uk

Belmount Hall ★★★★

An impressive Georgian house, recently renovated but still in part owned by the National Trust (it was donated to them by Beatrix Potter as part of her portfolio of properties around the Lakes). The sheer size of the place means that the majority of its business is dedicated to weddings or large parties. Individuals can, however, book during the week, with a minimum of three bedrooms for a two-night stay.

Outgate, Ambleside.
Tel: 01539 436373.
www.belmount.net

Winder Hall ★★★★

There are seven guest bedrooms in this family-run yet impressive 17th-century manor house. Each room is decorated to perfection with either brass, iron or four-poster beds, and all are en suite. Rates include afternoon tea with cake, scones and sandwiches, and other facilities include a jacuzzi, communal lounge with open fire, and lovely gardens. Information packs and packed lunches for walkers can be arranged. Evening meals consist of a five-course menu using local produce such as lamb or trout.

Low Lorton, Cockermouth.
Tel: 01900 85107.
www.winderhall.co.uk

EATING OUT

Log House Restaurant ★★

Something of a landmark in the area as it's located in a wooden Norwegian building, nevertheless the food here has won awards in its own right. Although the chef is a New Zealander, the culinary influences are Mediterranean, with dishes such as crayfish and chorizo warm salad. Simple and unpretentious, but fresh and delicious.

Lake Road, Ambleside.
Tel: 01539 431077.
Open: Tue–Sat 5–11pm.

Lucy's on a Plate ★★

Proprietor Lucy Nicholson has several establishments in the area, including a cookery school, but this is the original and best known. The evening menu changes nightly, while the daytime menu focuses on lighter salads and sandwiches. Those with a sweet tooth might enjoy the Pudding Nights, held on the first Wednesday of each month, with sample tastings of six different desserts.

Church Street, Ambleside.
Tel: 01539 431191.
Open: daily 10am–9pm.

Stampers Restaurant ★★

As you enjoy your speciality steak in the cellar room of this long-established restaurant, you can summon your own muse as you ponder that Wordsworth apparently wrote some poems here. Other highlights include local game and smoked fish.

The Old Stamphouse, Church Street, Ambleside.
Tel: 01539 432775.
Open: Tue–Sun noon–3pm & 7pm–midnight.

Jerichos ★★★

One of the most acclaimed restaurants in the national park, serving dishes such as black pudding and chorizo risotto and roast Gressingham duck in Madeira sauce (although seasonal produce is key so

the menu changes accordingly). There's also an excellent, well-thought-out wine list. Reservations recommended.
Waverley Hotel, College Road, Winderemere.
Tel: 01539 442522.
Open: Apr–Dec Tue–Sun 6.45–11pm; Jan–Mar Tue–Sat 6.45–11pm.

Borrowdale Gates Hotel ★★★★

The restaurant of this country house hotel is popular with locals for its well-prepared, locally sourced menu. Try the rack of lamb with ginger beer gravy, finished off with a classic Cumbrian sticky toffee pudding. The hotel also offers a delicious afternoon tea.
Grange-in-Borrowdale, Keswick.
Tel: 01768 777204. Open: daily noon–midnight.

Holbeck Ghyll ★★★★

Within this renowned hotel is a Michelin-starred restaurant in the panelled dining room or, in good weather, on the terrace – both with wonderful views of Windermere. Dishes include loin of venison with pumpkin purée or

squab pigeon with Madeira gravy. There's also a six-course fixed-price gourmet menu.
Holbeck Lane, Windermere.
Tel: 01539 432375.
Open: daily noon–3pm & 7pm–midnight.

ENTERTAINMENT

The Bitter End

A truly traditional English pub, but with a difference. It also houses its own tiny brewery. There's also a small food menu that focuses on locally reared beef.
15 Kirkgate, Cockermouth.
Tel: 01900 828993.
www.bitterend.co.uk

Dog and Gun

One of the most attractive pubs in town, with oak beams and an open fire in winter. Don't be alarmed if you see money tucked away in gaps in the walls – locals do this as donations for the Keswick Mountain Rescue team that has its base here. Plenty of real ales and homemade food menu.
2 Lake Road, Keswick.
Tel: 01768 773463.

Royal Oak

Something of a local institution, this is a beautiful 17th-century pub that has retained all the original architectural features such as oak beams. There's also a pretty beer garden surrounded by flowers in the summer.
Church Street, Ambleside.
Tel: 01539 433382.

Theatre by the Lake

The best-known entertainment venue in the Lake District has a year-round programme of dance and drama, as well as staging several annual festivals (*see p138*).
Lake Road, Keswick.
Tel: 01768 774411.
www.theatrebythelake.com

Zeffirelli's

One of the most popular cinema complexes in the Lake District, with four screens showing the latest releases. There's also a restaurant and a jazz bar on site, all of which makes for a fun night out.
Millans Park, Compston Road, Ambleside.
Tel: 01539 433845.
www.zeffirellis.com

SPORT AND LEISURE

Cockermouth Golf Club

This 18-hole course not only offers fine golfing facilities, but you can take in the breathtaking views of Bassenthwaite Lake as you try for a hole in one.
Embleton, Cockermouth. Tel: 01768 776941. www. cockermouthgolf.co.uk

Country Lanes

If you fancy seeing the Lake District from a bicycle saddle, this is the place to come to hire top-of-the-range mountain bikes, as well as helmets and any other cycling equipment.
Windermere Station, Windermere. Tel: 01539 444544. www. countrylaneslakedistrict. co.uk

Derwent Water Marina

One of the best and most popular places within the national park for all kinds of watersports, from sailing to canoeing to waterskiing. Equipment is for hire and tuition is also available.
Portinscale, Keswick. Tel: 01768 772912. www.derwentwatermarina. co.uk

Hawkshead Trout Farm

A haven for anglers, this fully stocked farm offers both boat fishing and riverbank fishing. Catches are limited according to the permit purchased at the farm, but is usually between two or four fish per bag. Further fishing can be done, however, provided that the catch is returned to the water.
The Boathouse, Hawkshead, Ambleside. Tel: 01539 436541. www.hawksheadtrout.com

High Adventure

One of the most romantic and atmospheric ways to get to grips with the Lake District landscape is to take a hot air balloon flight and gently drift over the lakes and fells, ending with a champagne toast on landing. Flights are, however, weather-dependent.
Rayrigg Road, Bowness-on-Windermere. Tel: 01539 447599. www.high-adventure.co.uk. Closed Nov–Mar.

Lake District Sheepdog Experience

A fascinating day out (over 12 years of age only) to learn how border collie sheepdogs are trained to help herd the flocks that are so intrinsic to the area.
Seathwaite, Duddon Valley. Tel: 01229 716235. www.lakedistrictsheepdog experience.co.uk

Low Wood Watersports Centre

More watersports available here, as well as an indoor climbing wall and various other activities. Equipment and instruction are supplied, if required.
Low Wood, Windermere. Tel: 01539 439441. www.elh.co.uk

Windermere Canoe Kayak

Primarily a place from which to hire canoes or kayaks; however, there are also two-day courses available for beginners.
The Boathouse, Ferry Nab, Windermere. Tel: 01539 444451. www. windermerecanoekayak. com

NORTH CUMBRIA

ACCOMMODATION

IBIS Carlisle ★

A real budget option in the centre of the city.

Rooms are air-conditioned, if a little sparse and impersonal, and there is Internet access and an on-site car park.

Botchergate, Carlisle.
Tel: 01228 518000.
www.ibishotels.com

The Tranquil Otter ★

These seven lakeside lodges take their name from the otters that make their home in the waters here. Each of the self-catering lodges is fully equipped and even has its own boat, while some also boast outdoor hot tubs. The area is a private nature reserve so is ideal for bird watching and many other outdoor activities.

The Lough, Thurstonfield, Carlisle.
Tel: 01228 576661. www. thetranquilotter.co.uk

Lakes Court Hotel ★★

Convenient to both the station and the motorway, there are 70 guest bedrooms available in one of Carlisle's main hotels. All the usual facilities are available, including Internet access in each room, and

there are also family rooms. As well as a formal dining room, there is a piano bar where snacks can be served.

Court Square, Carlisle.
Tel: 01228 531951.
www.lakescourthotel.co.uk

High Houses ★★★

With views across to the Lakes, the Solway Firth and even Scotland, on a good day, this restored farmhouse is a breathtaking place to stay. Limewashed walls, cobblestone floors, inglenook fireplaces and four-poster beds all add to the atmosphere, and the dinner menu comprises game (pheasant, partridge) that is shot on the farm itself. The bathroom facilities are shared, but as there are only three guest rooms, this is a small price to pay.

Snittlegarth, Ireby, Wigton.
Tel: 01697 301759.
www.highhouses.co.uk

Crosby Lodge Country House Hotel ★★★★

Set in an early 19th-century house built to resemble a castle and with beautiful landscaped

gardens, this is a very special place to stay. Communal areas include a grand hall with chaise longues and a light-filled bay windowed drawing room. The 11 guest bedrooms are all decorated with antiques, large beds and grand upholstery, without being fussy. The scarlet-painted dining room has a fine reputation, serving dishes such as chateaubriand. Everything about this place is memorable.

High Crosby, Crosby on Eden, Carlisle.
Tel: 01228 573618.
www.crosbylodge.co.uk

Crown and Mitre Hotel ★★★★

With its grand staircase and panelled ceilings, this large hotel still evokes the atmosphere of the turn of the 20th century. There are 98 rooms in total, including one suite and some family rooms, and the executive rooms include wireless Internet access. There's also a bar, restaurant and 24-hour room service available.

English Street, Carlisle.
Tel: 01228 525491.

www.crownandmitre-hotel-carlisle.com

The Weary Inn ★★★★

Despite its name, there's nothing 'inn-like' about this place – rooms have all the luxuries associated with 5-star hotels: flatscreen TVs and DVD players (even in the bathrooms), bathrobes, Egyptian cotton sheets and power showers and spa baths. The award-winning restaurant serves dishes such as local pheasant.
Castle Carrock.
Tel: 01228 670230.
www.theweary.com

EATING OUT

New Mills Trout Farm ★

While primarily a tearoom specialising in homemade cakes and pastries, savoury dishes such as soup (also homemade) are available. There are wonderful views that are worth the visit even if you're not interested in the fishing (*see pp144–5*).
Brampton.
Tel: 01697 741115.
www.newmillstroutfarm.
net. Open: Tue–Sun
10am–5pm.

Vivaldi ★

Plenty of Italian favourites here, from pasta to pizza to fresh grilled fish dishes, in a restaurant decorated in a modern take on country house style.
30 Lowther Street, Carlisle.
Tel: 01228 818333.
Open: Mon–Sat
noon–11pm.

Alexandros ★★

Traditional Greek favourites such as stifado, moussaka and baklava all feature on the menu here but there are also more unusual dishes such as their popular grilled tiger prawns wrapped in bacon.
68 Warwick Road, Carlisle.
Tel: 01228 592227.
Open: Tue–Sat noon–2pm & Mon–Sat 5.30–10pm.

Teza ★★

There's no hint of flocked wallpaper in this very modern and sleek Indian restaurant, and the food is innovative and freshly prepared. Traditional tandooris and curries are available as well as lighter meals, such as roti bread stuffed with minced lamb, which would constitute 'street food' on the subcontinent.
4 English Gate Plaza, Botchergate, Carlisle.
Tel: 01228 525111.
Open: Tue–Sun
noon–midnight.

ENTERTAINMENT

The Brickyard

The main live music venue in Cumbria, dedicated entirely to promoting new music, usually by local bands.
14 Fisher Street, Carlisle.
Tel: 01228 536708.
www.brick-yard.com

Cassa

One of Carlisle's more trendy venues, the bar has live DJs on Friday and Saturday nights. Alternatively, the cellar bar is a more relaxing experience.
4 Botchergate, Carlisle.
Tel: 01228 593000.
www.cassabar.co.uk

Club XS

Cumbria as a whole is rather lacking in nightclubs but this is one of the new arrivals on the scene. There are two dance floors: upstairs is chart music; downstairs is more serious dance tracks.

12 West Walls, Carlisle.
Tel: 01228 544282.

The Sands Centre

Touring West End productions, renowned stand-up comics, classical music concerts and rock concerts are all part of the varied programme at this popular arts venue. There is also a fitness centre onsite.

A7, Carlisle.
Tel: 01228 625222.
www.thesandscentre.co.uk

Vue

The chain group of cinemas has a base in Carlisle with seven large screens showing all the latest blockbusters and releases.

50 Botchergate,
Carlisle.
Tel: 08712 240240.

SPORT AND LEISURE

Carlisle Racecourse

A fun day out if you fancy a bit of a flutter on the horses on race days. There are also plenty of conference and party facilities here for hire.

Durdar Road, Carlisle.
Tel: 01228 554700.
www.carlisle-races.co.uk

New Mills Trout Farm

Both fly and bait fishing are available here, with rods and other equipment on hire if required, as well as tuition for novice anglers.

Brampton.
Tel: 01697 741115.
www.newmillstroutfarm.
net

EAST CUMBRIA

ACCOMMODATION

Blue Swallow Guest House ★

A clean and comfortable, conveniently situated guesthouse with seven rooms and a substantial full English breakfast served in the basement dining area.

11 Victoria Road, Penrith.
Tel: 01768 866335.
www.blueswallow.co.uk

The Manor House ★

This Georgian manor house has now been converted into a comfortable bed and breakfast. Rooms (including one family room) are nicely furnished and retain their original beamed ceilings, and there's a guest lounge and

breakfast room, where the owners prepare a full English breakfast to your requirements.

Mellbecks, Kirkby Stephen.
Tel: 01768 372757. www. manorhouse.netfirms.com

Woodclose Caravan Park ★

The winner of various tourist awards, this 3.5ha (9-acre) campsite has pitches for caravans supplied with electric hook-ups and a separate field for tent pitches. There's also a shop, an Internet café and a children's play area.

Chapel House Lane, Kirkby Lonsdale.
Tel: 01524 271597.
www.woodclosepark.com

A Corner of Eden ★★

If ever a bed and breakfast lived up to its name, this one does. Set in a converted listed farmhouse within acres of countryside, it has a cosy lounge, a hall equipped with umbrella stand and coat rack, and rooms with open fireplaces and beautiful cast iron beds; it almost feels as if you're in a private home. Although the four rooms are not en suite there are two luxurious bathrooms for guests. There is also an honesty bar and breakfast is served in the beautiful beamed dining room with long mahogany table.

Low Stennerskeugh, Ravenstonedale, Kirkby Stephen.
Tel: 01539 623370.
www.acornerofeden.co.uk

Tufton Arms Hotel ★★

While this building has been a coaching inn since the 16th century its décor is very much in the style of the Victorian era and all the plush elegance that goes with that. However, modern touches apply where they are needed, such as in the sophisticated en-suite bathrooms, complete with cosy dressing gowns.

Market Square, Appleby-in-Westmorland.
Tel: 01768 351593. www. tuftonarmshotel.co.uk

The Sun Inn ★★★

A lovely 17th-century inn that has retained its traditional bar, whitewashed exterior, and original stonework and beams, while adding modern luxuries such as duvets and flat screen TVs. There are 11 rooms in total, all en suite, and a highly acclaimed on-site restaurant.

6 Market Street, Kirkby Lonsdale.
Tel: 01524 271965.
www.sun-inn.info

Appleby Manor Country House Hotel ★★★★

A lovely converted 19th-century manor house that now offers 31 guest bedrooms, traditionally decorated, and plenty of original architectural features in the public rooms, such as oak panelling and stone carvings. Dining is available in either the Oak Room, or in summer in the bright conservatory or outside on the patio.

Roman Road, Appleby-in-Westmorland.
Tel: 01768 351571.
www.applebymanor.co.uk

Shap Wells Hotel ★★★★

Step back in time to the Victorian era with the grand entrance and plush lounge of the Shap Wells Hotel. The rooms are slightly dated in décor for the price, but are clean and comfortable and are all en suite. The dining room serves a very traditional English menu, such as roast beef and trifle.

Shap. Tel: 01931 716628.
www.shapwells.com

EATING OUT

Mango ★

An eclectic mix of Caribbean dishes, such as jambalaya, Mexican fajitas and Italian pizzas with friendly service and a relaxed atmosphere. The restaurant does not have a licence to sell alcohol but you can bring your own wine (for a small corkage fee).

Fell House, Shap.
Tel: 0845 0945716.
Open: Thur–Sun noon–2pm & 5–10pm.

Upfront Gallery Restaurant ★

A lunchtime-only vegetarian venue serving delicious quiches, pastas and soups, and some mouthwatering desserts and cakes. Outside seating is available in good weather.

Unthank, Penrith.
Tel: 01768 484538. Open:
Tue–Sun 10am–5pm.

The Highwayman Inn ★★

In business since the 18th century, this traditional inn has made itself a reputation for its food, with dishes such as fish pie and suckling pig. There's also a superb cheese board that specialises in cheeses from Cumbria and the neighbouring counties of Lancashire and Yorkshire. Plenty of locally brewed beers on offer, too.
Burrow, Kirkby Lonsdale.
Tel: 01524 273338.
Open: daily noon–11pm.

The Martindale Restaurant ★★★

For what it lacks in architectural charm, the menu at this hotel restaurant more than makes up for with its strong emphasis on locally sourced produce. Try the crab bisque, beef with a blue cheese sauce, or the much loved local staple, Cumberland sausage.
North Lakes Hotel and Spa, Ullswater Road, Penrith.
Tel: 01768 868111.
Open: Mon–Fri

noon–1.30pm &
7–9.30pm, Sat
6.30–9.30pm, Sun
7–8.45pm.

Sharrow Bay Country House Hotel ★★★★

One of the region's most acclaimed restaurants, and supposedly the birthplace of that popular dessert, sticky toffee pudding. Lamb with sweetbreads and sea bass with wild mushrooms are typical of the menu that is changed according to seasonal availability.
Lake Ullswater, Penrith.
Tel: 01768 486301. Open:
daily noon–midnight.

ENTERTAINMENT

The Rheged Centre

This unique grass-roofed building is home to seven cinema screens as well as various exhibitions, shops, cafés and more.
Redhills, Penrith.
Tel: 01768 868000.
www.rheged.com

SPORT AND LEISURE

Active8 Adventure

The primary focus here is tuition for rock climbing and scrambling, but there are plenty of other adventures, too,

such as coracle sailing, paintballing and survival skills.
Station House, Ullswater Road, Penrith.
Tel: 01768 892105. www.
active8adventure.co.uk

Rookin House

Pony trekking, go-karting, quad biking, clay pigeon shooting and paintballing are just some of the varied activities available at this long-established adventure centre. All activities, however, do need to be booked in advance.
Rookin House Farm, Troutbeck, Penrith.
Tel: 017684 83561.
www.rookinhouse.co.uk

Sunsoar Paragliding

If you've ever wanted to feel like a bird taking to the skies, paragliding may be the sport for you. Sunsoar offers a variety of courses with highly experienced instructors, although all courses are subject to weather conditions to ensure safety.
South Road, Kirkby Stephen.
Tel: 0870 1997343.
www.sunsoar-paragliding.
com

SOUTH CUMBRIA

ACCOMMODATION

Crooklands Hotel ★

Set in a lovely ivy-covered building, the Crooklands Hotel offers 30 recently renovated en-suite rooms with light and airy décor. There is a bar with open fire or outside tables in summer and a restaurant that is locally popular for its carvery for Sunday lunch. Good value for money.
Crooklands, Kendal. Tel: 01539 567432. www.crooklands.com

Candlewyck Barn Bed and Breakfast ★★

The main barn room of this bed and breakfast is set in a converted candle factory and has been lovingly converted into luxury accommodation, full of light and tasteful contemporary décor. There are also rooms in the main house. In addition there are on-site stables, so keen horse riders can even bring their own horse to stay, too.
Old Hall Road, Ulverston. Tel: 07830 341200. www.candlewyck.co.uk

The Duke of Edinburgh Hotel and Bar ★★

Completely refurbished in 2006, this long-standing hotel has lost none of its charm but has had a stylish overhaul in both the public rooms and the bedrooms. En-suite bathrooms, for instance, feature roll top baths as a nod to the Victorian heritage, but all in pristine modern settings. The bar, with its comfortable leather seating, prides itself on local ales and is popular with locals.
Abbey Road, Barrow-in-Furness. Tel: 01229 821039. www.thedukehotelandbar.co.uk

Highgate Hotel ★★

Set in a lovely 18th-century house in the centre of the town, you can enjoy a bit of history while making use of the modern facilities that have been included in the rooms, including tea- and coffee-making equipment.
128 Highgate, Kendal. Tel: 01539 724229. www.highgatehotel.co.uk

Low Graythwaite Hall ★★

The exterior of this bed and breakfast may be picture-perfect 16th-century architecture, but inside the bedrooms are right up to the minute, with leather-covered sleigh beds, pale carpets and sleek finishes. There's also a converted farmhouse on site offering self-catering accommodation for up to five people. There's an indoor pool and gym, and boat moorings at Windermere.
Graythwaite, Newby Bridge. Tel: 01539 531676. www.lowgraythwaitehall.co.uk

Castle Green Hotel ★★★★

Set in wonderful grounds, the traditional exterior of this hotel belies the elegant modernity that has been applied to the interior spaces. Pale wood and bright colours are everywhere, and beds are dressed with luxurious duvets. The restaurant focuses on local seasonal produce while the on-site pub serves local beers. There's

also a leisure area with pool, sauna and gym.
Castle Green Lane, Kendal.
Tel: 01539 734000.
www.castlegreen.co.uk

Damson Dene Hotel ★★★★

A place to be pampered in, with a full leisure centre with indoor pool, spa and sauna as well as various treatments such as massage and aromatherapy on offer. The hotel is also set in lovely landscaped gardens that make for a nice stroll, and rooms are traditionally decorated with plush furnishings.
Crosthwaite, Kendal.
Tel: 01539 568676.
www.damsondene.co.uk

Grange Hotel ★★★★

Victorian splendour abounds here, from its reception area with marble floor and chandelier, to the canopied beds and plush furnishings of the bedrooms. There's also a leisure centre with elegant indoor pool and beauty treatments on offer.
Station Square, Grange-over-Sands.

Tel: 01539 533666.
www.grange-hotel.co.uk

Swan Hotel ★★★★

If you're really in the money you can even arrive here in your own helicopter, as there is a helipad in the grounds! For the less flash, it's a pleasure simply to soak up the atmosphere and location of this beautiful hotel: the style throughout is a clever mix of traditional and contemporary.
Communal areas include a lounge and a library, while the elegant rooms all have wireless broadband and even children's toys, if required. There are two restaurants, a bar and a spa area with jacuzzi, sauna and full-size indoor swimming pool. Children are made particularly welcome and there is a children's play area in the grounds.
Newby Bridge.
Tel: 015395 31681.
www.swanhotel.com

EATING OUT

1657 Chocolate House ★

Chocoholics will be in heaven in this specialised shop and café, which

serves 14 different types of chocolate cake and 18 different chocolate drinks, both hot and cold. To add to the atmosphere, the waiting staff dress in 17th-century costume, reflecting the age of the building (hence the name).
54 Branthwaite Brow, Kendal.
Tel: 01539 740702. Open: Mon–Fri 10am–5pm, Sat 9.30am–5pm.

Cortez ★

Fantastic paellas of meat or fish, as well as tapas dishes such as battered squid or meatballs in red wine, bring customers back to this popular Spanish restaurant time and again.
101 Highgate, Kendal.
Tel: 01539 723123. Open: Mon–Sat noon–3pm & daily 5pm–midnight.

Bridge Street Restaurant ★★

Pure contemporary dining here, in both the simplicity of the food and the bright décor with modern art touches. Try black bream with scallops, or roast beef with thyme dumplings. There are two fixed price menus

of either two or three courses to choose from.
1 Bridge Street, Kendal. Tel: 01539 738855. www. bridgestreetkendal.co.uk. Open: Tue–Sat noon–2pm & Tue–Thur 7–9pm, Fri & Sat 6.30–9pm.

Danny's Restaurant and Café ★★

Chef-owner Danny is Romanian and the cuisine here is based around Eastern Europe such as goulash and dumplings. A welcome change if you're tired of English hot pots and pies.
36 Kirkland, Kendal. Tel: 01539 722009. Open: Wed–Sun noon–2pm & 6.30–10pm.

Newmoon Restaurant ★★

Contemporarily decorated with an equally modern menu – try the crab brulée or the silver mullet fillet. There's a shorter, cheaper menu at lunchtime and a good wine list, including dessert wines.
129 Highgate, Kendal. Tel: 01539 729254. Open: Tue–Sat 11.30am–2.15pm & Tue–Fri 5.30–9pm, Sat 6–9.30pm.

The Punch Bowl ★★

Classic dishes, beautifully prepared, such as Hot Pot (a traditional meat stew originally from Lancashire) or belly of pork, are the theme here, all served in an elegant modern-style dining room with pale wood floors and leather chairs.
Crosthwaite. Tel: 01539 568237. Open: daily noon–11pm.

Rustique ★★★

A fusion of British and French cooking is served here. The fish stew is delicious, as is the pork fillet with black pudding mousse.
Brogden Street, Ulverston. Tel: 01229 587373. Open: Tue–Sat noon–2pm & 7–9pm.

L'enclume ★★★★

A Michelin star-winning restaurant under the guidance of chef Simon Rogan, and probably the best place to eat in Cumbria. The menu is based on the sensory effect that flavours have on each other, such as cep ravioli with maple syrup or skate with pomegranate and avocado – it may sound a little bizarre but the results are delicious.
Cavendish Street, Cartmel, Grange-over-Sands. Tel: 01539 536362. Open: Sat & Sun noon–1.30pm & daily 6.30–9.30pm.

ENTERTAINMENT

Brewery Arts Centre

Set in an historic brewery building, there is a variety of entertainment on offer here year-round, from theatre to music to film. There's also a café with outdoor terrace and a restaurant.
Highgate, Kendal. Tel: 01539 725133. www.breweryarts.co.uk

Canteen Comedy Club

From 7pm onwards every Saturday night, both local and national comedy acts take to the stage to entertain the crowd.
Canteen Media and Arts Centre, Michaelson Road, Barrow-in-Furness. Tel: 01229 822113.

Castle Inn

A charmingly pretty traditional pub decorated with hanging baskets on the outside and a list of real ales behind the bar, such as Jennings. Good pub menu, too.
13 Castle Street, Kendal. Tel: 01539 729983.

Coronation Hall

Affectionately known as 'the Coro' this impressive Victorian building plays host to a wide range of events, from classical and rock music, to touring theatre, opera and ballet companies.

County Square, Ulverston.
Tel: 01229 588994.
www.corohall.co.uk

Watermill Inn

A lovely country pub noted for its own microbrewery and 16 different ales on tap. There's an outside terrace for warm weather and a simple food menu of pub favourites such as ploughman's lunch (bread and cheese platter).

Ings, Kendal.
Tel: 01539 821309.
www.watermillinn.co.uk

Ye Olde Fleece Inn

The oldest pub in Kendal, dating from 1654, on the site of a former slaughterhouse, all of the original features have been maintained. There's an open fire in winter and a simple but well-prepared menu of pub dishes such as steak and ale pie.

Highgate, Kendal.
Tel: 01539 720163.

SPORT AND LEISURE

Lakeland Climbing Centre

At 18m (59ft) high, the indoor climbing wall here is the largest in Cumbria and an ideal way to learn how to rock climb before venturing outside for the real thing. Outdoor courses, however, are also available.

Unit 27, Lake District Business Park, Mint Bridge, Kendal.
Tel: 01539 721766.
www.kendalwall.co.uk

Lakeland Mountain Ventures

Rock climbing, abseiling, canoeing and mountain biking are just some of the activities on offer with this company, either as a day adventure or for longer trips including overnight camping.

84 Windermere Road, Kendal.
Tel: 01539 741318. www.lakelandmountainventures.co.uk

Murthwaite Green Trekking Centre

Even if you've never been in the saddle before, you can enjoy a leisurely horse ride along the beach with these rein- lead trips led by experienced guides. All rides, whether short or long, must be booked in advance.

Silecroft, Millom.
Tel: 01229 770876.
www.murthwaitegreen.co.uk

Treks and Trails

Walking is the most popular activity in the Lake District, but sometimes it is more pleasurable to be guided by experienced leaders, who not only navigate the landscape expertly but also offer information about the area en route.

17 Dove Nest Lane, Endmoor, Kendal.
Tel: 01539 567477.
www.treksandtrails.co.uk

WEST CUMBRIA

ACCOMMODATION

Crookhurst Farm ★

There are two self-catering options here, within a working farm environment – the farmhouse can sleep between 10 and 12 people – or in the adjacent cottage for two to three people. There are wonderful views of the coast and the accommodation is fully equipped with items such as TVs and washing machines.

Bowscale Farm, Allonby, Maryport.

Tel: 01900 881228.

www.crookhurst.com

Fiddleback Farm ★

There are only two guest bedrooms in this bed and breakfast, but it is a unique place to stay. So named because the building was built in the shape of a fiddle (violin), inside the whitewashed walls perfectly highlight the original oak beams. The rooms are stylish and well equipped, with sofas and chairs as well as comfy beds. Evening meals are available if ordered in advance. Excellent value for money for a very memorable stay.

West Woodside, Wigton.

Tel: 01697 342197.

www.fiddlebackfarm.com

Moresby Hall ★★★

There are currently four guest bedrooms (with more planned in the near future) at this beautiful listed 17th-century country house, decorated with four-poster beds and traditional

furnishings alongside mod cons such as en suite power showers and satellite TVs. There are also two on-site cottages for group bookings. The dinner menu is all homemade and changes daily. Winner of many tourism awards.

Moresby, Whitehaven.

Tel: 01946 696317.

www.moresbyhall.co.uk

The Pennington ★★★★

It's quite a shock to walk inside this traditional-looking building and find oneself in an environment that would look more fitting in New York City than a small Cumbrian village. Renovated in 2007, the hotel has been decorated in striking contemporary style, from the leather-clad headboards, to the luscious duvets to the flat screen TVs and DVD players.

Main Street, Ravenglass.

Tel: 01229 717222.

www.thepennington.co.uk

EATING OUT

Gincase Tearoom ★

Set in the former corn-grinding building in what is now part museum, part

art gallery and part farm, this tearoom is decorated with various historic features including an original 18th-century range stove. Both savoury and sweet dishes are on offer using traditional Cumbrian recipes, such as tattie pot.

The Gincase, Mawbrey Hayrigg, Silloth.

Tel: 01697 332020.

www.gincase.co.uk.

Open: Feb–Dec Tue–Sun 10.30am–4.30pm.

Crosby Seafood Restaurant ★★

As its name would suggest, the freshest of fish and seafood is on the menu here such as Solway Firth shrimps. Or simply go for that great British favourite, fish and chips.

32 Tangier Street, Whitehaven.

Tel: 01946 62622.

Open: daily noon–2pm & 5–10pm.

McMenamins ★★★

Making wonderful use of seasonal local produce, this is probably the best restaurant in town. The menu focuses on Cumbrian lamb and beef, particularly for Sunday lunches, as well

as truly fresh fish and seafood such as pan-fried sea bass.
Irish Street, Maryport.
Tel: 01900 819777.
www.mcmenamins.co.uk.
Open: daily noon–2pm & 6–9pm.

Zest ★★★
Even Tony and Cherie Blair have graced the dining room of this highly acclaimed restaurant, one of northern England's finest. There's also a sister restaurant, Zest Harbourside, which has the added benefit of coastal views.
Low Road, Whitehaven.
Tel: 01946 692848. Open: Wed–Fri 6.30–9.30pm, Sat 6.30–10pm.

ENTERTAINMENT
Ratty Arms
Railway enthusiasts can finish off a trip on the Ravenglass steam railway (*see p105*) with a pint of ale in this pub set in a former station. Various railway memorabilia decorates the walls.
Ravenglass Station.
Tel: 01229 717676.

Rosehill Theatre
Live music, theatrical performances, children's entertainment and a cinema are all part of this popular complex.
Moresby, Whitehaven.
Tel: 01946 692422.
www.rosehilltheatre.co.uk

The Vagabond
A very traditional pub that is well known in the area for its live folk, blues and acoustic music. It gets very crowded at weekends. Also serves a simple but well-prepared food menu.
9 Marlborough Street, Whitehaven.
Tel: 01946 693671.

Whitehaven Civic Hall
Rock and pop bands as well as comedians are regular fixtures on the civic hall's year-round programme. Recent performers have included the punk band The Jam.
Lowther Street, Whitehaven.
Tel: 01946 852821.
www.civichall.org.uk

SPORT AND LEISURE
Carol Climb
Both indoor and outdoor climbing instruction is offered here, as well as opportunities for abseiling and canoeing.
Low Gillerthwaite Field Centre, Ennerdale.
Tel: 01946 862342.
www.carolclimb.co.uk

Eclipse Leisure Centre
The largest ten-pin bowling centre in Cumbria is popular year-round. There are also various other indoor entertainment facilities such as one-armed bandit and other gaming machines, a pool table and a bar.
Derwent Howe Industrial Estate, Workington.
Tel: 01900 872207.
www.eclipse-bowling.co.uk

West Coast Karting
If you fancy a little bit of the thrill of a Grand Prix racing circuit, there's no better fun in an entirely safe environment than racing go-karts around this large indoor track.
Solway Trading Estate, Maryport.
Tel: 01900 816472. www.westcoastkarting.co.uk

Whitehaven Golf Course
One of the newer golf courses in Cumbria, this is an 18-hole course with the added bonus of great coastal views.
Red Lonning, Whitehaven.
Tel: 01946 591177.

Index

Acknowledgements

Thomas Cook Publishing wishes to thank MARK BASSETT for the photographs in this book, to whom the copyright belongs, except for the following images:

TREVOR DOUBLE 130

FLICKR/mick Tony Austin 38, 39, Edward (Deluxe) 49, Bay Photographic 67, Neil Boothman 109, 111, clurr 116, judepics 117, ahisgett 120, foshie 127, Leon Wilson 129, Steve Cadman 138, dumbledad 144

GETTY IMAGES/Val Corbett 63, Christopher Furlong 79, Cate Gillon 149

THE LAKES AQUARIUM 92

LEVENS HALL 103

MARY EVANS PICTURE LIBRARY 62

PICTURES COLOUR LIBRARY 13, 44, 54, 61, 85, 94

POPPERFOTO/GETTY IMAGES 38, 39

THE QUAKER TAPESTRY 90

THE THEATRE BY THE LAKE 139

WIKIMEDIA COMMONS/Davidberry 51 21, Cyberdemon007 77, Supergolden 81

WORLD PICTURES/PHOTOSHOT 121, 123, 124, 125

For CAMBRIDGE PUBLISHING MANAGEMENT LTD:
Project editor: Ros Munro
Typesetter: Paul Queripel
Copy editor: Jenni Rainford
Proofreader: Dick Lloyd Williams
Indexer: Karolin Thomas

SEND YOUR THOUGHTS TO
BOOKS@THOMASCOOK.COM

We're committed to providing the very best up-to-date information in our travel guides and constantly strive to make them as useful as they can be. You can help us to improve future editions by letting us have your feedback. If you've made a wonderful discovery on your travels that we don't already feature, if you'd like to inform us about recent changes to anything that we do include, or if you simply want to let us know your thoughts about this guidebook and how we can make it even better – we'd love to hear from you.

Send us ideas, discoveries and recommendations today and then look out for your valuable input in the next edition of this title.

Emails to the above address, or letters to Travellers Series Editor, Thomas Cook Publishing, PO Box 227, Unit 9, Coningsby Road, Peterborough PE3 8SB, UK.

Please don't forget to let us know which title your feedback refers to!